A CHILD PRISONER OF WAR
The Story of Thomas Ryan

Singapore 1942-45
Changi and Sime Road Camps

by

Christopher Ryan

HAKAWATI PRESS
HAWICK

Published by Hakawati Press, Hawick, Scotland

First published 2021
Copyright © Christopher Ryan 2021

All rights reserved
No part of this publication may be reproduced, stored in a retrieval system, or transmitted, in any form or by any means (electronic, mechanical, photocopying, recording or otherwise) without the prior permission of the author

For further information contact the author at
damascus_drum@yahoo.com

To Kate, Hilary, Nick and Perrine

1

LOOSE THREADS

My father was a travelling man. And his father before him. And his grandfather too on his mother's side, if the truth be told, a wandering Jew by the few accounts that sifted down the years, whispered rumour laid to rest in cold statement of fact following my father's death. But it was there to see as plain as the nose on my beautiful grandmother Sarah's face: Sephardim or Ashkenazi, who can say; cast up on Ireland's shore who knows when or how. Or, and there is no-one to disprove, perhaps even an Arab, for to look at her she could as easily have stepped out of the streets of Aleppo or Sidon, instead of Ashton Street, Liverpool 3. We never knew great-grandfather's name; he was not allowed to marry the good Irish Catholic girl that was my great-grandmother, but he left this seed of the great Jewish soul to grow and multiply in fertile Catholic earth upon the banks of the River Mersey. And well before this seed showed forth in the light of day as my grandmother Sarah, this good earth was tended by the quite Catholic man, Mr Barrett, enlisted to shore up my great-grandmother's precarious honour through a hastily arranged marriage.

Grandmother Sarah married at eighteen John Ryan, a rake, by whom she first bore a son, my father, Thomas, known first as Tommie, then Tommy, and later Tom. And during John Ryan's peregrinations of northern towns and the Scottish Borders as a travelling salesman – he only returned home when whatever he earned had been frittered away on women, whisky and games of chance -

Sarah bore him in addition a daughter, Molly and later Leo, a second son.

In the dark hours before dawn on Christmas Day in 1925 my father appeared, and the attending midwife was so thrilled that she cried out to my grandma's confusion, 'you must call him Noel', which was not at all the name Sarah wished for him. Yet, when his birth came to be registered, his name was written down as Thomas Noel, although the intended name was Thomas Christopher, by which name he was always known, and to which it was later changed by deed poll.

It became evident quite early on that Tommie Ryan's destiny lay in his being ever in transit in this world. One day, aged two years, so the story has come down to us, as Sarah was distracted dealing with a shopkeeper, the toddler Tommie wandered from the shop into the street and climbed up into the underside of a parked lorry, into the place where the spare tyre was kept. The lorry drove off and he was spotted some time later clinging onto the spare tyre miles away in another part of Liverpool. The police were called and the little wanderer was eventually returned to the frantic Sarah.

John Ryan was one among an unknown number of sons who were heirs to a large cobblers and surgical bootmakers business in Liverpool. Whether it was the marriage to a girl of dubious antecedence - there was no hiding my grandmother's dark-eyed East Mediterranean beauty – or on his own account due to his promiscuous attitude in financial and familial matters (whenever he was flush, he would buy a new suit and disappear, only returning when the money ran out) – when he died an untimely death sometime around 1940, the Ryans cut off all connection with Sarah, widowed young at thirty-three years, and her brood of three. Without even the sporadic contributions of her late husband John, things got so bad that when the bailiffs came round they took two of the four kitchen chairs, saying two would have to do. Although poor and uneducated - her reading and writing always remained fairly rudimentary - nevertheless she was a very attractive young woman with a quick wit and a good sense of humour, and she soon found work as a hotel barmaid.

Already by this time, shortly after the outbreak of World War II, John Ryan took Tommie out of school and sent him to work, in spite of the bright lad's having won entry into a respectable Catholic boy's school. In what is probably his final school report in September 1940, Head teacher Charles Taylor writes: 'His attendance has been regular and punctual. He works very well with average results; he is very willing, amenable to discipline and respectful.' and ends by saying 'I have found him to be quite honest.'

At the time the family were renting a small terraced house in Ashton Street, since demolished. The site now houses part of Liverpool University. Shortly after, when John Ryan had passed on in the summer of 1940, Sarah and the children moved to 101 Ponsonby Street, in Liverpool 8. Only later, after the infamous 1981 riots that began in nearby Granby Street, was the name Toxteth used for the area, and which became synonymous with a negative portrayal of Liverpool during the Thatcher era. The docks are about a mile away as the crow flies, down Upper Parliament Street. The house next door to 101 was bombed in the blitz and never rebuilt.

Ponsonby Street doesn't exist now. Well, the houses don't, at any rate. A tarmac strip runs between two rectangles of park grass connecting to the two parallel streets on either side, but all the buildings are gone bar one at the end where the street meets Granby

Street: a three storey brick corner shop, all boarded up with a sign by the former occupant Ken which tells us that 'Ken's moved to xxGranby St, call etc.' Opposite is 'Pakistan General Store', also boarded up, and nearby a modern-ish estate. A few blocks away is the grand Al Rahma Mosque and Liverpool Muslim Society. At the other end of Ponsonby Street, around the corner in Kingsley Road, is Our Lady of Lourdes and St Bernard Catholic Church.

This was a poor area then, and with no tv, and little material possessions to distract; there was a strong culture of street activities, with games of football and cricket played out in the street, and older boys and girls making banter and tentative liaisons. Tommie apparently was more interested in books than sport, or girls at that age. Whenever he and his sister were given any money, Molly would always buy sweets, but Tommie would buy a book. This was a habit he never lost in later life, and during our own childhood he was regularly joining bookclubs and always reading the latest novels, Graham Greene, Ian Fleming, Nicholas Montserrat, Alastair Maclean, in hardback, as well as modern history. He was a speed reader, and regularly finished off a novel over supper before going back out for evening surgery.

Released from the rigours of formal education onto the streets of Liverpool, young Tommie took up apprenticeships, first to a boiler maker, then to a cooper. From this latter's employ he was summarily dismissed: the story goes that he had recently seen the 1925 epic silent film, Ben-Hur, in which Ramon Novarro and Francis X Bushman fight it out in Hollywood's most famous chariot race. Unfortunately for Tommie, as he imitated his heroes with the cooper's horse and dray loaded with barrels and hurtled down Liverpool's

Lime Street, like so many charioteers in the film, he was unable to make the turn. The cart capsized and crashed, smashing the cargo of barrels in the process.

Having left school, and having failed to find satisfaction in either of his apprenticeships, with world war in progress, perhaps Tommie just got impatient. He was evidently a bright lad with an enthusiastic sense of adventure that would benefit from some curbing. Growing up in Liverpool, a crucial hub for the trans-Atlantic convoys, and living in such close proximity to the docks, it would have been surprising if Tommie's inclination had not led him to join the fight in a more practical way than building barrels or boilers. The sea was calling.

Unlike the armed forces which were rigorous in enforcing their minimum age requirements, the Merchant Navy, the 'fourth service', was desperately in need of men to fulfill the growing crewing requirements for vessels bringing essential supplies of food and arms from America. It was prepared to turn a blind eye to almost any person, within reason, who applied. The age limit was sixteen. Tommie had just turned fifteen when he fetched up before the hallowed portals of the Royal Liver Building to apply for employment with Canadian Pacific Steamship Company, at the time the biggest transportation company in the world, and a major carrier in the North Atlantic convoys. His 'Continuous Certificate of Discharge', the seaman's passport, gives his date of birth as 25 December 1924, a year earlier than that given on his birth certificate. His height at the time was five feet two inches. The photo in this document is of a good looking child, with a mop of curly dark hair and a serious and somewhat faraway look in his eyes. But so young, really just a child.

As a minor, Tommie would still have had to have a parent's or guardian's signature before he would be taken on. By what means did he persuade his widowed mother to release him upon the wild oceans of the world at such a tender age? Charm or subterfuge, who knows? Perhaps Sarah too had lost patience and thought it better to let him go. Or maybe she wept mother's tears at seeing him depart. Probably both.

Merseyside - that is, the docks of Liverpool and Birkenhead - was the major arterial link keeping the lifeblood of food and materials necessary for supplying the war effort. At this distance in time, some eighty years on, where now our world enjoys such sophisticated global transport and communications systems, with every real or imagined need delivered to our door at the click of a computer button, we must reorient ourselves in a much simpler world if we are to appreciate the problems facing an island nation beseiged by air and sea from life's principal necessities of food and shelter, and the means for its self-defence.

Over 90% of Britain's war supplies from abroad passed through the eleven miles of Liverpool's docks. As well as being Britain's busiest port, Liverpool also served as a base for the Royal Navy and the headquarters of the 'Western Approaches Command', a deep basement bunker with a seven foot thick concrete roof, right in the heart of the city's shipping business district and close to the docks. It was in this 'Fortress' that the planning and strategy for the Battle of the Atlantic took place, 24 hours a day, every day, from early 1941 until the end of World War Two.

Another factor may have contributed to Tommie Ryan's decision to go to sea. Since late August 1940 Liverpool had been suffering aerial bombardment from the Luftwaffe on an almost nightly basis. The blitz reached a peak in the first week of May 1941 when raids totalling 681 German bombers created mayhem as high explosive bombs and incendiaries rained down upon the docks and homes of Merseyside. It was a toss-up whether life was riskier on land or at sea. But at age fifteen, life is experienced in the moment. Death, in spite of the evidence surrounding one, doesn't impinge in the same way upon souls that have yet to make a mark in life. Youth has still to discover the myth of futures and tomorrows. Most likely it was the urge to get involved, to be with the big boys, to be doing something, that defined Tommie's choice to go to sea.

The winter of 1940-1941 in Britain was harsh. A major snowstorm hit the country between 18th and 20th January with snowdrifts ten feet deep in the Wirral. In such conditions, Tommie Ryan took ship as 'Cooks Boy' in the catering department aboard S.S. Beaverbrae. She was a relatively modern ship, built in Armstrong and Whitworth's Newcastle shipyards in 1928. Her six steam turbines produced 1,581 horsepower which drove twin propellers powering the ship at a top speed of fifteen and a half knots, twice the speed of a submerged U-boat. For this reason Beaverbrae did not travel as part of a convoy, being 'independently routed'. It would be a round voyage out of Liverpool to Saint John in New Brunswick, Canada. She was likely travelling out in ballast and returning with war supplies. Capable of carrying heavy general cargoes, in pre-war days Beaverbrae had carried dismantled German aircraft to Canada, and her sistership had transported the steam engine 'Royal Scot' on its deck, with eight carriages, to America and back. Her return cargo now would be food and military supplies of every description.

On the evening of 25th January 1941, the vessel put to sea. It was a pitch-dark night, two days short of the New Moon. In the docks of Liverpool, Birkenhead and Wallesey, all lights were extinguished according to the Blackout Regulations. It is not difficult to conjure the scene: skies dark with lowering cloud, the bitter winds, raw with snow and ice and spray ripping through one's clothes, and black waves buffeting inexorably like muffled bells of doom upon the steel plates of the ship's hull as tugs towed it out from the docks, and it sailed down between the protective banks of the River Mersey, blacked out from aeriel sight, into the wild North Sea.

It is a truth universally acknowledged that a single boy setting out upon a seaman's life must be in want of a strong order, a system of firm discipline, if he is not to fall by the wayside. Abandoned by father, now abandoning his mother, he could not have fallen under a more steady star by which to steer the unruly craft of his youth than the British Merchant Navy; and few more esteemed berths were to be had than on a ship of the distinguished Canadian Pacific Steamships. Aboard ship, Captain was God, and little Tommie Ryan found himself at the lowest of low positions, lower than which there is not, as the Cooks Boy. Although his status varied on future voyages, during his war service, he was never to relinquish this diminutive appendage of 'boy', until, many years later in his student years he was taken on as 'Assistant Laundry Man' for a month as a holiday job.

According to George Monk, who served as radio officer on Beaverbrae in 1940, she was a good ship. CPS was a good company which looked after its crew better than many lesser shipping lines. Unlike in older ships, where the crew had been crammed up for'ard in the foc'sle, or astern in the 'poop deck', all accomodation for crew and officers was amidships. The food, says Monk, was 'surprisingly superb'. Did later Ryans enjoy some kind of atavistic descent of good taste through Tommie's early experiences in CPS's catering department? Hard to say, but there can be no doubt that, in helping to prepare food for a ship's complement of eighty or so, after the deprivations of poverty and rationing at home, he would have taken the opportunity to encourage his meagre five foot two inches to greater heights. He did top out eventually at five foot eight inches, in spite of later hardships, and always had a taste for good food.

This first voyage went without incident. No U-boats, no surface raiders, no aerial attack. On reaching Canada, while the ship was being loaded, he may have had some shore leave. Perhaps he made contact with his cousins who lived in Nova Scotia. In any event, setting foot on foreign soil for the first time, grateful to have arrived safely after such a dangerous crossing, this country must have made a strong impression on the young cook's boy. In the late 1960s he did work for a few months in Canada, and even contemplated a new life in this part of the world, though in the end it came to nothing. At his age, and size, it is unlikely that he was introduced to the low life world of seamen's bars and houses of ill repute, such as there may have been in this small port city. More likely he was taken under the wing by some responsible rating and kept clear of such dens of iniquities. At any rate, at the end of the voyage it appears that he acquitted himself well for his 'Report of Character' is stamped 'VERY GOOD' for both ability and general conduct.

2

ATTACK ON THE BEAVERBRAE

Tommie's second voyage might have been a repeat of the first. Beaverbrae slipped her moorings and departed Liverpool in late March, under the guardian aegis of the shore batteries, negotiating the anti-submarine nets and other defences, its course carefully plotted to avoid the explosive chainmail of coastal minefields which protected Britain's Western Approaches. Its route would take it north passing the Isle of Man and the Scottish island of Islay to starboard, then towards Iceland, before heading west for the quickest crossing to Canada's north east.

A few days out, as a grey dawn was beginning to break over a churning North Atlantic swell, Beaverbrae was steaming somewhere a little south of the Faroe Islands. Suddenly overhead, out of the thick, low cloud, a deep rumble was heard. Then barely three hundred feet above, a German Focke-Wulf Condor broke cover, cannons and machine guns blazing shells in its path towards the ship.

The Focke-Wulf Condor was Germany's long-range reconnaissance bomber, and next to the U-boat, the adversary most feared by the Merchant Navy. A large four-engined plane, it had originally been developed as an international airliner, making the first non-stop Berlin to New York flight in 1938. Now it was a death machine, equipped with three machine guns and capable of carrying a bomb load of over 2,000 lbs.

Beaverbrae, though alone, was not entirely unprotected. She was a 'Defensively Equipped Merchant Ship', and was armed with a 4-inch gun, and a 40mm Bofors gun situated aft, and two 'Hotchkiss' 6-pounders (an obsolete gun from the late 19th century), as well as a stripped down Lewis gun on the bridge.

Even as the first stick of bombs was still falling, the Lewis gun at the stern of the ship was pouring lead into the plane overhead. The Condor scored a double hit on the afterdeck with two large bombs, destroying the masthead, the derricks, opening up the steel deck and penetrating deep inside the ship where they exploded, causing immense damage. Pipes burst in the engine room, the escaping steam scalding men badly, but no fatalities were suffered. Fires broke out and spread quickly and were soon out of control.

The Condor turned to make a second pass. Although the deck fires were making it difficult for gunners to reach the Bofors in the stern, the gun crews on the bridge were waiting now, and as the bomber flew over, they let fly with the two Hotchkiss and the machine gun. Visible tracers could be seen passing through the body of the plane, and its bombs fell harmlessly into the sea. Again the Condor pressed home its attack, but again to no avail. By the time the German plane approached on a fourth bombing run, the Bofors gun was firing steadily, causing the enemy to swerve away. It headed off, vanishing into the grey heights of cloud and did not return.

The noise, the smoke, the fires, the screaming of the burned sailors as they were brought up from below deck - where was Tommie Ryan in all of this? Fifteen years old and all at sea without a doubt, and experiencing a baptism of blood and fire. Perhaps he was helping relay buckets of sand to douse the fire, or had he been told to assemble at the lifeboat station? Looking down he noticed that his trouser leg was torn and soaked in blood. A piece of shrapnel had nicked his leg, a scallop slice from his calf muscle maybe two inches long. Nothing serious, but initiation nonetheless, and he carried the pale scar proudly.

Meanwhile the fires were spreading. The crew did their best, but the damage was too great. It became clear very quickly that they could not contain the growing conflagration. At 8.45 am, just under an hour after the first attack, Captain B. L. Leslie gave the order to abandon ship. A coded message was radioed to Western Approaches Command back in Liverpool, giving their position, 60'12" north, 09'00"west, and the ship's condition, and all eighty-six members of Beaverbrae's company, including the injured, took to the life boats.

All day they sat there in the cold Arctic winds, tossing about on the ocean, watching their former home burning away and hoping no enemy planes would spot the black smoke billowing, for it was not unknown for lifeboats to be strafed. Luckily being attacked so close to Britain meant that a reasonably quick rescue was possible. A plane of the RAF did pass over and drop some supplies to the beleaguered sailors, then shortly after 5pm two Royal Navy destroyers arrived on the scene like knights in grey armour, and soon had everyone on board. Captain Leslie hoped that they would be able to tow Beaverbrae, albeit a burning wreck, back to port, but he was dissuaded of the idea as she would make a slow moving target for U-boats. Beaverbrae was left to sink.

As much as Tommie would have been relieved at the sight of those two warships careening through the waves to their rescue before the coming of night, even more thrilled he would have been boarding a ship of the line, a real man-o'-war of the Royal Navy. What fifteen-year-old boy would not have been impressed by the confident military efficiency which extended the hand of compassion coupled with the hand of might, and swept those poor bedraggled seamen, cold, exhausted and far from home, out of the jaws of the deep and sped them to safety. Such experiences would have been seminal in influencing his joining the RNVR after the war, and subsequently the Royal Australian Navy.

One of these maritime knights was HMS Tartar, illustrious namesake of an 18th century Royal Navy frigate. There are many tales to tell of this heroic ship's wartime adventures. Surviving numerous scrapes in many theatres of conflict in World War Two she became known as 'Lucky Tartar', and carried scars as well as collecting twelve battle honours, by the end of the war. A couple of weeks prior to rescuing Tommie Ryan and his eighty-five shipmates, Tartar had taken part in Operation Claymore, a commando raid on the Norway's Lofoten Islands which succeeded in destroying the herring oil factories, the product of which was used in making munitions. In the course of the raids, Tartar boarded a German trawler, *Krebs*, and captured codebooks and a set of rotor wheels for the German code machine Enigma, enabling the codebreakers in Bletchley Park to read German messages for some time afterwards. Two months later Tartar took part in the hunt for and sinking of the German battleship Bismark. Tartar's First Lieutenant at the time was the writer and BBC broadcaster Sir Ludovic Kennedy. Three months later, in August 1941, HMS Tartar carried Churchill on the final leg of his journey returning from his Atlantic Charter meeting with President Roosevelt. The other destroyer, HMS Gurkha, which also took part in the Lofoten raid, was far less lucky . She was sunk in early 1942, barely a year after she had been commissioned. Tartar and Gurkha had been on duty protecting minesweepers in the Western Approaches when they answered Beaverbrae's distress call.

      With the crew of Beaverbrae safely aboard, the destroyers steamed through the night, reaching Scapa Flow the following morning at 9.45. Scapa Flow is a deep natural harbour in Orkney, the group of islands just beyond the northern tip of mainland Scotland. It had been the base for the British Grand Fleet in the First World War, and now served as haven for the Home Fleet which protected the convoys to Murmansk. From here the crew were brought to Thurso where they boarded the train back to Liverpool. Once again, my father's Certificate of Discharge is stamped 'VERY GOOD' for both ability and general conduct.

After the terrifying experience of being attacked and sunk at sea, Tommie Ryan might well now have decided to find other, notionally safer, land-based employment. But in spite of his brief time as a seaman, this sinking had established something in him. Tenuous though his footing may have been at this stage, nonetheless he could now count himself in the world of men - men who were doing something useful, commendable, honourable even. Maybe the choice wasn't so difficult: either to continue living at home in Liverpool and be treated as a child, surviving on rations, perhaps find a job in the docks, hard, dangerous work at any time, now with the added risk of regular raids by German bombers; or return to sea and be treated as a young adult, with regular meals and a warm bed to sleep in, and see the world. Yes, there was always the risk of being sunk, but he'd lived through one battle, he'd been wounded yet he'd been lucky, rescued by a lucky ship. And luck favours the brave.

3

TOMMIE AND THE EMPRESS

Tommie's return to Liverpool at the beginning of April 1941 coincided with the arrival in port of one of the great ocean liners of the day, the Canadian Pacific's Empress of Asia. Launched in Glasgow in 1912, she was already an old lady with an illustrious career behind her when she berthed at Gladstone Dock to be refitted as a troopship. The bridge was reinforced, a wide range of anti-aircraft and anti-submarine weaponry installed, including a six-inch gun, rockets and depth charges.

During the First World War, the Empress of Asia had been requisitioned and armed with eight 4.7" guns and manned by the Royal Navy initially to fight German interests in the Far East. Later in the war, under Canadian command, she carried Canadian troops to the Western Front, bringing the survivors home again after the Armistice in 1918. Between the wars she fulfilled her original purpose as a premium luxury liner on the Pacific Ocean run between Far East ports and Canada.

This service was briefly interrupted in August 1937 when the Empress was called upon help evacuate 1,300 British nationals during the infamous Battle of Shanghai, which followed the Japanese invasion of China. The horrors of this battle are graphically portrayed in Kazuo Ishiguro's novel, 'When We Were Orphans', dramatically foreshadowing later events in Singapore.

Then in 1940, while sailing towards Yokohama, there was the curious incident of the student pilots of the Imperial Japanese Navy who mistook the liner for a target and dropped their practice bombs. One pierced through two decks and burst in the kitchens by the vegetable store, injuring a number of Chinese crew, without doubt a further foretaste of things to come. A 'statement of profound regret' was issued by the Japanese government.

Now, in 1941, the Empress had been requisitioned again as a troopship, and was taking on a new British and Empire crew, as its mostly Chinese peacetime crew had opted to return home to China. The catering department on an ocean liner is necessarily a large affair, akin to the staff of a very large hotel, and Tommie Ryan was soon signed up, this time as 'Officer's Boy'.

In order to have some idea of the kind of tasks that Tommie and his fellow ratings would have faced in the catering department of a big liner, it is necessary to look at the whole picture of how a British merchant ship was, and to some extent still is operated. The crew is divided into three departments:

> i) *the deck department*, which involves mostly working in the operational functions of the ship, including cargo loading and unloading, exterior maintenance such as 'swabbing' the deck, maintaining winches and cranes, cleaning the holds and all the 'outside' parts of the ship, as well as mooring, steering and lookout duties and assisting with navigation.

ii) *the engine room*, which as well as maintaining and running the engines and machinery, includes the electrical and safety systems of the vessel, water pumps, plumbing, and fuel systems. In coal-fired ships, such as Empress of Asia, it would also include the stokers, without doubt the most physically demanding job of all.

iii) *the catering department*. This completely parallels most of the jobs in the hotel industry, and includes purchasing, loading and storing of food, the preparing of meals by the cooks with all the ancilliary kitchen duties including the washing up, the laying of tables, serving of meals and clearing by the stewards and the 'boys', as well as normal housekeeping duties such as cleaning all the corridors, accommodation and leisure areas, as well as being responsible for cleaning cabins, and providing linen and doing the laundry.

After Tommie's brief period as cook's boy in the modestly crewed (eighty-six) Beaverbrae, a job akin perhaps to working at the bottom end of the scale in a small restaurant ashore, duties in a big passenger liner would have been far more specific and delineated. As an Officers' boy, as he was on this first voyage in Empress, he would have seen to the ship's officers' dining needs, working together with another Officers' boy, the young T. Trust, under the strict eye of the Officer's Steward, a Mr E. Larkin. They would have brought up the food and drink for the ship's officers, and in time learnt to serve at table under Mr Larkin's supervision, and been responsible for the perfect laying out the linen tablecloths, the silver and glassware, all spotless and polished, and the removal of all this at the end of meals. And there weren't just three meals a day, for it would be necessary also to see that the officers coming off watch during the night were amply nourished. In all, as with most duties at sea in wartime, it was a round the clock job.

With the refit completed, 2,000 troops were embarked - Yorkshiremen of the infantry regiment, The Green Howards - destined for Egypt. With a Royal Navy escort, Empress of Asia departed Liverpool on 24 April 1941 and steamed up the west coast to Glasgow where the various components of the convoy, number WS 8A, were gathering in the Clyde, this being the only place capable of providing sufficient anchorage for large convoys to assemble. The convoy comprised fourteen vessels, including five ships which would soon branch off east to Gibraltar as part of Operation Tiger to supply Malta. One of these five, Empire Song, didn't make it. It hit a mine in the Strait of Sicily and sank with the loss of fifty-seven tanks and ten planes.

The initial stage of the voyage would bring the troops to Suez, via Cape of Good Hope, arriving early in June, as reinforcements for the North Africa campaign. This long diversion was necessary because a direct route via the Mediterranean, at the height of the Seige of Malta, would have been suicidal.

An escort of destroyers, the battle cruiser HMS Repulse and light cruiser HMS Naiad accompanied the convoy until 2nd May when they detatched to escort the five military supply vessels to Gibraltar. It must have been a thrilling sight for young Tommie, and given a great sense of reassurance to the whole convoy to witness these powerful warships running alongside; most especially the famous capital ship, Repulse, with its massive fifteen inch guns, two twin-turrets fore, and one aft, and bristling with lesser armaments, torpedoes, as well as four seaplanes launched from catapults. Ten-inch thick steel armour plate protected the conning tower, and most of the armour was at least six inches thick. It had been the fastest large warship in the world at the time of its launch in 1916, and although coal fired, it could still manage a top speed of thirty one knots. But she was an old ship, and destined, like the Empress herself, to meet her end in the dark and not so far off days of the Fall of Singapore.

A new escort of four destroyers with the cruiser HMS Mauritius and an armed merchant cruiser joined the convoy to give protective cover on the next leg to the first port of call, Freetown in Sierra Leone, arriving 9th May. This West African state grew out of a settlement initially founded around 1787 by freed slaves from Britain, the United States and Jamaica. From 1808 until 1961 it was a British Crown Colony, and served as the base for the Royal Navy's West Africa Squadron whose original task was to halt the slave trade. During World War Two Freetown was the base for escort and rescue operations for convoys in this section of the Atlantic. For convoys it was also a bunkering station where the ships took on coal or oil, as well as fresh water. Because Freetown was only an anchorage, and had little in the way of docks, the coal had to be loaded by hand from lighters.

It is unlikely that Tommie would have been allowed ashore, and was probably only able to glimpse the sandy shores of Sierra Leone and the colourful streets of Freetown from the deck of Empress in his rare off-duty moments. Nevertheless, the heat of the African sun after the bitter winter days would be acting as a leaven in him, expanding feelings of possibilities that had little hope of fruition in the cold of nothern climes. In spite of the dangers, perhaps by now the young lad from the streets of Liverpool was developing a taste for the open road, for travel and adventure, wherever it might lead. However it would be many years before he would be able to give free reign to these notions.

Convoy WS 8A sailed from Freetown five days later on Wednesday 14th May, at 10 am. Under the watchful eye of the newly commissioned light-cruiser HMS Mauritius, they steamed at a steady 13.7 knots for Capetown and Durban in South Africa.

Around this period in the war, Britain and her allies were losing upwards of a third of a million tons of ships to German U-boats and bombers every month. A breakthrough in the 'Enigma' code in June 1941 saw these losses reduced from 2 million tons January to June, to around a third of that figure in the second half of the year. Sadly, with more and more U-boats being commissioned, and now hunting in 'wolf packs', losses in 1942 increased to record levels. Only the diversion of energy by the Nazis towards the ill-fated (for Germany) Russian front saved the British war effort.

The convoys travelled in a very definite formation, grouped on a wide grid in rows vertically and horizontally. Imagine the sea as a chess board, each square perhaps half a mile wide, and in the centre of each square, a merchant ship. All maintaining, or trying to maintain, the same speed, the same distance from its neighbour, while the escort ships took positions around the outside. The smaller destroyers or corvettes would move around the merchantmen like sheepdogs managing a flock, intervening if the formation was getting ragged, or if ships were too close to each other. The convoy maintained the speed of the slowest vessel. If U-boats were seen or suspected, the convoy would ziz-zag, again in formation, in an attempt to make it difficult for a torpedo attack to have success. It was a constant, wearisome, hour by hour, minute by minute occupation for the ships' officers to keep watch, against U-boats and for their own position, while maintaining correct speed and direction. And if the weather was rough, which it invariably was in the northern and southern regions of the Atlantic, mercilessly rough and cold, no one got any rest, even when off duty. For the men in the engine room, the stokers, the firemen, unseen and unseeing, but hearing the vessels passage through the battering seas, noting the commands from the bridge to increase or decrease speed, monitoring the movements of the steering gear, sweating in the stink and heat of boilers, it was doubly stressful, and may have accounted for the constant mutterings and occasional mutinies among the engine room crew aboard Empress of Asia during its war service.

The further south they sailed, the worse the weather became. Capetown and Durban were reached after about a fortnight. On arrival at the Cape, due to the number of ships moving in the area at this time, the convoy split between the two ports. Delays for repairs and bad weather meant a week's stay in South Africa. On 31st May five vessels detatched themselves from the group, forming a smaller convoy, and headed on north through the Indian Ocean, arriving in Aden at the head of the Red Sea on 6th June. Once in the Red Sea, the ships proceeded independently to Suez. Empress of Asia, which had been delayed in Capetown due to a dispute with the Engine Room crew, didn't reach Durban until 5th June and arrived in Suez somewhat later. After two months at sea, the two thousand men of The Green Howards were disembarked in the blinding heat and sand of the Sinai on one side of the Canal with Africa and the land of Pharoahs and the Nile on the other. They were speedily loaded into trucks and disappeared to their Egyptian encampments, while the crew of the Empress began to restore the ship for its new complement of passengers.

The situation for the Allies in the Middle East in mid-1941 was precarious. The battle lines of the desert war drifted back and forth, sometimes to the Allies advantage but more often not. But by the time Tommie's convoy arrived in Egypt some successes against Italian forces meant there were a lot of prisoners to be removed into safe-keeping far from where they might cause trouble in the future. For the Empress of Asia, this meant embarking around a thousand Italian Prisoners of War for POW camps in South Africa. In addition provision had to be made for the evacuation of around three hundred civilians and military personel being redeployed to different theatres of war.

One of the officers taken on for the voyage to Durban was the young Prince Phillip of Greece, who had joined the Royal Navy in 1939 and had been serving on convoy protection duties in the Indian Ocean up until this time. As Officers' Boy, it is quite possible that Tommie may have waited on the future consort to the British Monarch.

By a strange twist of fate, during the 1963 Royal Visit to Australia by Queen Elizabeth II and Prince Phillip, Tommie, by now Surgeon Lieutenant-Commander Thomas Ryan, was invited by an old friend, Captain 'Nobby' Clark of the escorting destroyer HMAS Anzac, to join this ship as Medical Officer. In February and March that year they escorted the Royal Yacht Britannia for six weeks circumnavigating Australia on a voyage of over 10,000 miles, and this time Tommie definitely did meet the Prince. Whether either became aware that their paths had already crossed under such very different circumstances is not known.

Empress of Asia steamed safely back to Durban, and after disembarking its Italian POWs and its distinguished sub-lieutenant, crossed the Atlantic, and bunkered in Trinadad before reaching New York. After affecting some repairs the Empress sailed on to Halifax to pick up two thousand Canadian troops, and then on 16th September 1941 she joined a large convoy for Liverpool. Tommie left the ship in Liverpool on 29th September. He had been at sea for over five months, he had visited four continents, crossed three oceans and his horizons had been expanded beyond his expectations.

4

JOURNEY INTO FEAR

When Tommie Ryan was paid off after this long voyage, his Certificate of Discharge was stamped with a mere 'GOOD' for ability, and a questionable 'Decline to Report' for general conduct. What mischief did this young boy get up to in the fleshpots of Durban or Suez? Did Trinidad rum lay him low? Or perhaps the bright lights and big city led him astray in New York. Or had scouse wit - or scouse lip, as some might say - not been fully appreciated by the officers in the upper decks? It would be surprising if a young lad, in earnest effort to gain experience of the world, and in order to keep up with his shipmates, did not get into a bit of trouble from time to time. However, those three words which appear so ambiguous to us could in fact be quite damning for a British merchant seaman. It categorically indicates serious displeasure on the part of the ship's master. Tommie Ryan had definitely blotted his copybook. Only two 'VERY GOOD's on the next voyage would go some way to restoring his damaged reputation. A second 'DR' could mean the end of his career at sea. But let us not be too quick to condemn. Whole crews have been known to receive a 'DR', as it is called, with even the innocent suffering along with the guilty. It seems that the British Merchant Navy conforms to the Ottoman notion of, 'Let the green wood burn with the dry.'

Canadian Pacific was always considered a top company to work for, but discipline was perhaps stricter on a passenger ship than on a normal freighter. The person responsible for discipline was the Master at Arms, a kind of seaboard policeman, who could and would dole out fines for misdemeanours. While flogging was no longer a practice, when a ships boy is only paid thirty shillings a month, a fine, possibly as much as five pounds, would seriously curtail his adventures next time ashore.

Whatever offence, if any, Tommie had committed, while evidently it was not so heinous as to prevent him being re-employed for Empress of Asia's next voyage – it was wartime after all and necessary at times to overlook most venial offences – Tommie was no longer to enjoy the clean and airy spaces of the upper decks. Since that *'first disobedience'* as 'Officers' Boy', the Almighty, manifesting in the form of Captain Smith now had him, like Milton's Adam,

'hurled headlong flaming from th' ethereal sky,
With hideous ruin and combustion, down
To bottomless perdition, there to dwell
In adamantine chains and penal fire'

and he became 'Engineers' Boy', bussing between the hot, steamy kitchens and the even hotter flames of the coal-fired boilers of the engine room.

Convoy WS 12Z was to be another trip via the Cape of Good Hope carrying troops to the Middle East. Sailing from Liverpool on 12th November 1941 north through the Irish Sea, the Empress of Asia made rendezvous with fourteen other ships off Oversay, a small islet off the Scottish island of Islay on 13th November. The group then proceeded west over the top of Ireland before heading south.

The convoy had a variously changing escort of as many as half a dozen destroyers or corvettes all the way down through the South Atlantic. Continuing round the Cape and to the East it was accompanied by the battleship *HMS Royal Sovereign*, a grand old warrior from WW1, with a massive range of armaments including eight 15-inch guns and fourteen 6-inch guns.

Among the ships were many great liners of the day. As well as two other Canadian Pacific ships, Duchess of Bedford and Empress of Japan (its name was later changed to Empress of Scotland when Japan entered the war), also sailing were the P&O liner SS Narkunda, acting as 'Commodore', the lead ship, placed front centre in the convoy, and seven other passenger liners. Painted in camouflage grey, and flanked by their formidable escort, the fleet must have presented a formidable sight, especially when viewed under the dark cloud of war.

One of the troops aboard Empress of Japan writes that in Freetown, reached 24/25 November: *"the men were not allowed off the ship and were to spend a hot and sticky night aboard. They would lean over the rails and throw coins for the native boys to dive for from their canoes. Some of them soon refused to dive for pennies thrown, so the cruel humoured of the troops threw half pennies or farthings wrapped in silver foil over the side. This act had every native boy diving madly into the depths to get to the coin first, much*

to the delight of the soldiers above. These coins were to become known as 'Glasgow tanners' by the natives."
(from 'Life of Riley' by Ted Marriot - http://www.far-eastern-heroes.org.uk/Life_of_Riley/index.htm)

Only a brief stop was made to take on bunkers, and the convoy weighed anchor on 26th November. Two days out of Freetown, Empress of Japan was hit by a torpedo which failed to explode. Vigilance throughout the fleet was heightened following this nerve-wracking incident.

As well as the daily shift, or 'watch' – there were three eight-hour watches in the day – young recruits when not at work would spend time in training, learning the seaman's craft, as well as fire drills, lifeboat drills etc., even learning to tie knots.

The convoy reached Durban without further incident on 18th December at night. With the city lights blazing, for there was certainly no danger of air-raids and so no black-out in force, Durban was a welcome sight to the thousands of crew and troops who had passaged endless nights upon the sea in darkened ships.

Here the crew received news of the bombing of Pearl Harbour, Hawaii, by the Japanese, and the subsequent entry of the United States into the war. Japanese intentions with regard to British interests in the Far East also became evident, and the need to reinforce Allied forces in the region, in particular in Malaya and Singapore, became imperative. After long weeks cooped up at sea, the troops were billeted on shore and given much needed exercise and fresh air, while in distant offices of the Allied military command the destinations, and thus the destinies, of tens of thousands of men were being rearranged.

Meanwhile the crew were given shore leave. According to another young member of the Empress of Asia's catering crew, Leonard Butler, the South Africans were extremely hospitable to the sailors, taking them on tours of the countryside and feeding them fresh fruit and chocolate, luxuries virtually unheard of in England under rationing. For Tommie and his fellow shipmates this was a brief taste of paradise before the descent into the unknown darknesses that lay ahead.

After a week's rest much of the convoy pressed on, splitting into three units off Mombasa. Empress of Asia, however, stayed over Christmas Day in Durban, where the ship received new orders to make its way up the east coast of Africa and then across the Arabian Sea to Bombay (Mumbai), which was reached on 15th January 1942.

The troops on Empress of Asia had originally been destined for the North African campaign and had no training in jungle warfare. Once disembarked in Bombay, a new set of troops, 2,235 in all, jungle-ready, so to speak, came aboard. With a crew of 416 including 25 gunners, there were a total of 2,651 persons who set sail on what was to be the Empress' final voyage.

The convoy that left Bombay on 23rd January 1942 comprised five ships: Empress of Asia; Felix Roussel, manned mostly by Free French Navy seamen; Plancius, the headquarters ship of the Dutch forces in the Far East; the English troopship City of Canterbury; and the liner Devonshire (which later took part in the D-Day landings). It was led by an escort cruiser, HMS Exeter, famous for her part in the Battle of the River Plate. Each of these ships have a unique and interesting story to tell in their own right.

There are numerous accounts in military records, including the Captain's report, as well as personal diaries and memoirs of soldiers and seamen, of the events which followed Empress of Asia's departure. One can only conjecture from this distance the atmosphere that must have pervaded the ship. A stop was made in Ceylon (Sri Lanka) and the soldiers were given shore leave. In the minds of the men, being given shore leave so soon after departing Bombay, it was evident that they would soon be in battle, and although it had yet to be announced, most believed they were headed for Singapore to help stop the Japanese advance through Malaya. As for the crew, again they were sailing into unknown, and decidedly unfriendly waters.

From Ceylon they joined another convoy of eight ships also heading towards Java, or Batavia as it was then called. Still part of the Dutch East Indies under Dutch control, Indonesia was yet to emerge as an independent nation. Under normal, peacetime conditions, the route to Singapore would have been across the Bay of Bengal and down the Malacca Strait, between the Malay Peninsula and the east coast of Sumatra. But with the rapid advance of the Japanese, this would have put the fleet well in range of Japanese bombers. So they passed further south and then up through the Sunda Strait, which separates the islands of Java and Sumatra, passing close by the famous volcanic island of

Krakatoa, and then back north along the coast of Sumatra to reach Singapore through the Banka Strait.

5

STRAIT IS THE GATE

On 4th February 1942, as the rest of the convoy headed into Batavia, the five Singapore-bound ships sailed up into the Banka Strait. They were little more than twenty four hours short of their destination. The weather was sunny, hot during the day, and the sea calm.

The Banka Strait is a narrow stretch of water about a hundred and twenty miles long, varying from between ten to twenty miles wide. To the west lies the island of Sumatra, to the east, Banka Island, reputedly the setting for Conrad's novel 'Lord Jim'. It lies just below the Equator, a couple of hundred miles south of Singapore.

From muddy shores of mangrove swamps with deep green jungle behind, the land rises in the distance to low volcanic hills of scrub-covered rock of over a thousand feet. Because of the offshore mudbanks, navigation is through a narrow, defined channel which made it necessary for the convoy to travel in single file. The escort cruiser HMS Exeter led the way, with Empress of Asia, the only coal-burner, and therefore the slowest in the convoy, bringing up the rear. As they entered the Strait, vigilance was high, and every extra gun was brought out and manned as a precaution against possible attack by Japanese planes coming in low over the hills.

Reports from the ship's Master, Captain Smith, tell us that they were steaming at around 12 ½ knots, and expected to reach Keppel Harbour in Singapore the next afternoon. At around 11 o'clock in the morning the enemy showed themselves. High up in the deep blue sky, well out of range of the ship's guns, a flash of silver wings alerted those on deck to more than a dozen Japanese planes flying in a wide 'V' overhead. From the belly of one fell a mass of bombs, all directed towards Empress of Asia. From such a height accuracy was not to be expected. In the event the ship escaped direct hits, but the bombs exploded far too close for comfort, spraying the decks with water and shrapnel. Two of the lifeboats were damaged. It is believed that the bombs were incendiary types. The stokers, although not endangered at this stage, once they heard bombs going off, they fled the engine room. Perhaps their collective nerves, stretched to breaking point time and time again over the past year, now finally broke. They did return to their posts after a while, but by now the ship had lost speed. It was deemed necessary to enlist volunteer stokers from among the troops to ensure against a repetition of this event

The planes flew off, leaving the men of the Empress to contemplate their fate. Now that the Japanese knew their whereabouts it was only a matter of time. The two fast ships in the convoy, Plancius and Devonshire, went on ahead independently. By now a number of other Allied warships had arrived to escort for the final leg to Singapore, among them HMS Danae, and two sloops, one each of the Australian and Indian navies, HMAS Yarra and HMIS Sutlej.

It was a long night. Dawn broke silvery and light on the morning of 5th February and the day came on with blue skies and high clouds over a placid sea. From on deck one could make out Singapore in the distance, evidenced by the looming shroud of black smoke reaching high above the land. And Empress of Asia, her crew, the troops, all moved slowly but inexorably towards their joint and varied destinies. The water was smooth as a mirror, reflecting back the light and heat of the day.

Through the night the ships had reached halfway up the coast of Sumatra and were entering the clear channel between the minefields protecting the entrance to Singapore. Their intended destination, the Keppel Docks on the east side of the island, was still some way off. The convoy, still moving in single file, slowed to around five or six knots, preparing to take on board pilots for the last few miles of this long voyage.

Everyone was waiting, expecting something to happen. But this did not lessen the shock when the attack finally came. First a squadron of around twenty four two-engine bombers arrived, high up like the previous day, passing over, noting the convoy's position and then disappearing into cloud. Shortly afterwards, at 11 am, they returned. Not *en masse*, but in ones and twos and threes, descending to around 3,000 feet before releasing their bomb loads. The planes attacked from every direction. It was such a coordinated effort it was as if the enemy had spent the time since the previous day's reconnaissance raid planning this effective strategy. In a few short weeks the Japanese invasion force had captured most of Malaya, taking its airstrips from where it enacted a blitz upon Singapore, effectively neutralising the air defenses both of the island and the ships that were now attempting to bring relief and reinforcements.

Actions stations had been sounded at the first sight of planes. When they reappeared, every gun on every ship opened up. Bombs began to fall all around the Empress of Asia. It seemed that the Japanese had singled out this ship for special attention. The first two waves of planes dropped their bombs wide of the Empress, but then a single plane flew over, scoring a direct hit on the starboard side, near the most forward of her three funnels. A fire started and a fire crew immediately set about attempting to bring the blaze under control. Another bomb penetrated the rear of the Officers' Lounge and continued into the deck below. The lounge had been full of men, and in the flash of its passing and subsequent explosion below, one officer was killed and two badly injured. Now the ship poured out its own pall of smoke as the fires grew.

The escort cruiser HMS Exeter travelling close by the Empress now found itself a target of a concerted bombardment. She managed to fight off her attackers by her speed and manoevrability, coupled with the firepower of her anti-aircraft batteries, and came off unscathed˙.

The marauding bombers renewed their attack on the Empress, moving slowly now beneath her dark shroud of smoke. For two hours the ship withstood this sustained bombardment,

---

˙ Less than a month later, on 2 March 1942, HMS Exeter was sunk in action against the Imperial Japanese Navy off Java.

but the flames were spreading. The first bomb to hit had damaged the water pipes, and although the pumps worked at full speed, no water reached the fire hydrants around the ship. Fire extinguishers, fire buckets, axes - everything possible was put to use but the crew were unable to deal effectively with the spreading conflagration. The troops, who had originally been kept inboard at the beginning of the attack, were now mustered fore and aft. The engine room and stokehold began to fill with smoke from the fires in the accommodation areas in the upper decks, and so had to be evacuated. By 11.30 am, just half an hour since the attack began, the Chief Officer reported that the fires were completely out of control. Fire and smoke filled the air while all around came the mad, terrible, deafening noise of war as every gun aboard the Empress fired at will, while the escort ships wove in an encirling dance, their anti-aircraft guns giving some degree of protective cover from the Japanese planes.

Because of the smoke from the fires, maintaining a presence on the bridge became impossible. The captain decided to move the ship, which was by now making very little headway, near to a little island lighthouse called Sultan Shoal, and drop anchor. Confidential documents were either burnt or disposed of over the side of the ship and the bridge was abandoned, the men climbing down by rope onto the fore-deck of the ship as the area below was aflame. It was midday and they were about eleven miles west of Singapore. The Japanese attack ended less than an hour after it had begun. The pilots, having unloaded all their bombs, just flew away. Perhaps also, seeing the ship on fire and hardly moving, they believed their mission was accomplished.

By now the whole mid-section of the Empress was ablaze. It was not possible to lower many lifeboats due to the smoke in the boat deck and in any case many of the lifeboats were on fire. But significant areas fore and aft towards the ends of the ship were undamaged, and here the crew and troops were crammed together. Somewhere in their midst was a small, little more than five feet two inches tall, Engineers' Boy by the name of Tommie Ryan. One can almost hear him muttering, ' To be sunk once was unfortunate, to be sunk twice is just plain carelessness.'

It is impossible now to believe that the earlier 'friendly fire' incident of Japan's 'accidental' bombing of Empress of Asia on her way to Yokohama in 1940 was anything but a calculated practice run, searching out the ship's weaknesses in advance of an well-prepared invasion plan of British interests in the Far East. At the very least it had been an early warning shot across the bows.

Having given instructions that the canon shells for Empress's six inch gun were to be dumped overboard to prevent further explosions, at around 1 PM, Captain Smith gave the order to abandon ship. What followed was in retrospect, one of the most extraordinary rescues, among so many such, of the war. How to abandon ship with a complement of close to 3,000 men, with no lifeboats?

'By whatever means possible' appears to have been the order of the day. An Australian corvette, HMAS Yarra, then captained by Commander Hastings Harrington, (later to become

Vice-Admiral Sir Hastings Harrison, R.A.N., Chief of Naval Staff) performed a most extraordinary manoeuvre, nudging her bows right up against the stern of Empress of Asia. Soldiers and crew from the stricken ship were able to step directly onto the sloop's foredeck. In addition, Yarra's small boats, floats and rafts were lowered to aid in the rescue. Eventually the ship was so loaded with men, clinging from every available square inch of purchase, that as Commander Harrington pulled away, fearing for the stability of his ship, he gave orders that all hands were to sit down. In all it is estimated that around 1,800 men were taken off this way, outnumbering Yarra's own crew of 160 by more than ten to one. If little Tommie Ryan was among them, hanging on for dear life in some corner of the sloop's grey metal, it would not be the only time that he would be under Harrington's command. Years later, as Flag Officer Commanding HM Australian Fleet in 1959, Harrington was effectively Tom Ryan's ultimate commanding officer when as Surgeon Lieutenant Ryan he served in the Royal Australian Navy at HMAS Creswell that year. HMAS Yarra, for her part, ended her short but illustrious career under a different captain barely a month later, sunk by Japanese cruisers while escorting a convoy retreating from Batavia (Jakarta).

    Another Australian ship, the corvette HMAS Wollongong, stood forward of Empress of Asia, unable to come in close due to the steep overhang of the liner's bows, and assisted in rescuing the Master and the Ship' Engineer, the last to leave the ship, lowering themselves on ropes.

In the sick bay of the stricken vessel, patients were exiting via the portholes, directly into the sea. The calmness of the water was in complete contrast to the mayhem in the sky. The water was warm and many were able to swim to the shore of the nearby island of the Sultan Shoal Lighthouse. Small boats from surrounding escorts began to ferry people from the Empress, as well as some dinghies which had been dropped overboard, and relayed men from the ship to the island where they were picked up later. Many of the crew and troops left this way, by jumping into the sea, or lowering themselves on ropes. Because everyone had donned lifejackets as soon as the attack had started, even those unable to swim had a good chance of survival, as long as sharks didn't get them. Some clung to flotsam from the burning ship, and were carried away in the current. A tug arrived later and began to collect men from the sea, and from the island. Within two hours every man had been evacuated from the burning decks of the vessel and brought to safety in Singapore. Out of Empress of Asia's total complement of 2,651 men, only fifteen troops had been killed in the attack (one purportedly taken by a shark), and one crew member died.

The Empress of Asia came to rest in shallow water a mere ten miles short of the docks. Its blackened hull burned for days and days. All the stores and military ordnance, the tanks, guns and ammunition to defend this last outpost of the British Empire in the Far East were lost on the last ship in the last convoy to reach Singapore before it fell. The Japanese bombed it a number of times in the coming week, and it eventually sank, leaving its funnels still showing above water. Years later its rusting half-submerged hulk was towed out and sunk in deeper water.

By nightfall all the surviving ship's officers and crew, and the troops, had been brought ashore at Keppel Docks, the main dockyard in Singapore Island. Canadian Pacific's agents were at hand to attend.

Many of the deck and engine room crew were immediately assigned to other ships, taken on to crew unmanned vessels sitting in port to help with the civilian evacuation of the island that was, rather belatedly, now desperately underway. It was here that it was proposed that the entire Catering Department of the Empress should remain in Singapore to assist in the various medical establishments. The hospitals were already having to deal with a fast-growing number of cases, both the military wounded in the retreat from Malaya, from the many casualties caused by the Japanese bombing of the island in the past weeks, and from the inevitable battles to come. One wonders if there was any choice in the matter, or did these brave sons of the dying empire actually volunteer to a man. Perhaps Tommie and others had had enough of being sunk for the time being and felt it a safer bet to remain on terra firma. In any case, it would have been difficult, nay impossible, for a young lad washed up on this foreign shore to go against the tide of his peers and elders.

6

NARROW IS THE WAY

Japan's arrival into World War Two came gradually and by stealth. The 'Second Sino-Japanese War' began in July 1937, after seven years of encroachment in Chinese territory. In September 1940 Japan invaded Indo-China by land, sea and air. After a year consolidating its position it was poised to move further south. In two days in December the fate of South East Asia, extending down to New Guinea in the south, and Burma in the east, was sealed. The Pearl Harbour attack on 7th December 1941 effectively neutralised the US fleet in the Pacific for long enough to make possible seaborn landings the very next day in southern Thailand and Malaya with little opposition. Then, just hours after Pearl Harbour, early on 8th December, the Japanese bombed Singapore, the Phillipines and Hong Kong. That same afternoon the only remaining allied capital ships in the region, the battleship HMS Prince of Wales and the battlecruiser HMS Repulse, sailed from Singapore north towards the Gulf of Siam to meet the Japanese invasion fleet. On 10th December the ships were met by a force of 88 Japanese bombers, 34 of which carried torpedoes. In the ensuing battle, both British ships were sunk, leaving the seas in both the Western Pacific and around South East Asia under Japanese domination and opening the way for the taking of Singapore and the Dutch East Indies (Indonesia).

Singapore lies like an oval-shaped lozenge, a turtle on its back, just off the southern tip of the Malay Peninsula. About thirty miles at its widest, east-west, and nearly twenty miles north-south. The length of its north shore is separated from the Southeast Asian landmass by a narrow channel, the Johore Strait. This waterway is only a few hundred yards wide in many places, and easily swimmable. In 1942 the island was connected to the Malay Peninsula by a causeway, situated centrally on this north coast. In early February this carried a constant stream of refugees heading south out of Malaya to the supposed safe haven of Singapore: women and children, the families of plantation owners and civil servants, military wounded from the fighting, and in the last days, ragged military units effecting a 'tactical retreat'.

On the opposite side of the island, on the central southern shore, is Keppel Harbour. It is a stretch of water up to a mile wide running for roughly three to four miles separating the mainland of Singapore Island from two small islands, Brani and Pulau Blakang Mati (now called Sentosa Island) It is a natural deepwater harbour protected from open sea by the islands opposite. In early February 1942 the Keppel Docks were a scene of havoc and frantic activity. Amid the smoke and carnage pursuant on the incessant Japanese bombing raids, the last ships of the last convoys tied up at the wharves, unloaded their troops and cargoes, then immediately after filling up with evacuating civilians, they departed.

Singapore Town lay just behind the docks. From contemporary accounts it is apparent that for much of the

European civilian population at least, the inevitable was not yet seen as such. Bars were still open and people were out on the streets in the evening, keeping their spirits up, quickly making for air raid shelters when the sirens began and the bombs began to drop. The Raffles Hotel was still advertising dances, ice-cream sellers sold their wares from tricycle stands in the streets and newspaper vendors, strangely hopeful in anticipation of a last stand battle, and perhaps a British victory, called out the latest headlines, 'Good News! Japanese land on Singapore'. But as the week progressed the sense of doom thickened with the smoke covering the island due to the incessant air raids, and the first Japanese troops were reported to have crossed the Johore Strait. There was little left with which to defend the island; the troops were no longer able to organise efficiently as lines of communication were in complete disarray, the airforce was ineffective as most of the planes had by then been destroyed, and the naval vessels were now mostly at sea escorting the fleeing evacuation ships.

There is little to go on regarding Tommie Ryan's early days on the island. Accounts from other crew members relate that the 126 members of the Empress's catering department were given clothes on landing, then trucked up the Upper Serangoon Road five or six miles north of the town and billeted in an army camp at Bidadari, an old cemetery area, (where, incidentally, is buried an English sailor, Augustine Podmore Williams, on whom Joseph Conrad based the character of Lord Jim). The crew were kept in Bidadari camp for two days, during which time they were issued with rifles and told to get into trenches and form a second line of defence as an attack was expected that night. It appears that an over-zealous army officer, seeing the crew all in army fatigues, assumed they were there as part of the defence force. Few of the catering crew had ever held arms more dangerous than carving knives and meat cleavers, but orders were orders. The trenches were full of water up to their knees and they spent half the night there waiting. Needless to say, there was no attack.

Then some people from the Malayan Medical Services Corp arrived and brought the crew to the Singapore General Hospital. What awaited them here was a scene from hell. From rumours reaching Singapore of atrocities committed by the invading forces in the Malay Peninsula, the female nurses had been evacuated. The dead - some troops who had not survived their wounds, and some civilians who had died in the bombing - were literally piled up on top of each other in the morgue and hospital the corridors. The smell of gangrene and flesh decaying in the tropical heat was beyond foul. The men and boys from the Empress of Asia could do little as there was no water or food to give the surviving patients, but they helped where they could.

The brief siege of Singapore, the battles that ensued, and the ignominious surrender, are well documented. The end came just ten weeks after the first landings in Malaya, ten days since Tommie and his comrades had hauled up like drowned rats on the quay at Keppel Dockyard. Few would argue that the 'Fall' constituted Britain's worst military defeat. Churchill certainly felt it to be so, calling it 'the worst disaster and largest capitulation in

British history', while the facts, in hindsight, show the inevitable – that the war with Germany meant Britain was simply too overstretched to afford to release naval and air forces in sufficient numbers to effectively oppose the Japanese. The Atlantic Convoys were the real lifeline ensuring Britain remained free to wage war against the Axis forces in Europe, and as such nothing could be allowed to weaken the British position at home. So, after Pearl Harbour, only a token naval force, the muscle of which was quickly destroyed by the Japanese, was dispatched to the region. That the island didn't hold out longer is not surprising, as once the Japanese captured the water supply, further resistance would have been suicide.

But there is another factor. When taken in the global context, events of worldwide significance usually have their roots in, and are dictated by, the direction of the global will. The failure of the Gallipoli Campaign, the collapse of Communism, the Viet Nam war, Napoleon's march on Moscow, the repeated attempts to quell Afghanistan, all are situations which, when applying the question 'what if', we may find no viable alternative. Singapore, and by extension the hinterland of the Straits Settlements in the Malay Peninsula and Borneo, had represented the heart of Colonial ambitions in the region for over a century. It was inevitable in the grander scheme of the human/global evolution, that change must come, necessitating the removal of the old order. And evolution, be it in the Darwinian sense of the adapting of species, or in the development of the human potential, may also be seen as the manifesting in our world of the movement of a single, universal existence itself, right from the point of the 'Big Bang'. Such change appears inexorable, whether on the macro or microcosmic level. The 'how' is never pre-fixed.

The global will is a constant and perplexing oscillation between unity and multiplicity: single origin, one world, humanity with multitudes of forms of life, people, tribes, nations. A body with faculties, at once participating in a war between parts and sharing in a peace through agreement, the stretching and dividing of cells until reaching a moment of completion, then collapse and change. But peaceful agreement without recognising the essential non-reality of borders can only momentarily be total. Occasionally, when as a result of exhaustion, we put our guns on the ground and recognise the ultimate unity of our small wills, for an instant out of time, unity, true unity may reign. And in the meantime it is up to us, immersed since birth in this world of relativity, to learn to 'combine between the opposites' and perhaps to gain a little wisdom in seeing the order as compassion and allowing that to flow in us; then submitting, if but a little, to this essential movement of existence.

But what is true on the macro scale, has its correspondence in the micro. For Tommie Ryan, as for all involved in these global events, the change was inescapable, literally in his case. The first Japanese landing had taken place in the north-west of the island on 8 February. When the surrender took place on 15th February 1942, more than a 100,000 allied troops were taken prisoner. European civilian prisoners, which included British merchant seamen, numbered around 3,000. It also must not be forgotten, in our concern to record the journey of one unwitting foreign teenager upon Asian shores, the horror experienced by the resident Chinese population in the initial weeks, when anything from 25,000 to 100,000, mostly males between 18 and 55 years of age, were rounded up on charges of being anti-Japanese and summarily executed.. The official figure given by the Japanese is 5,000. Of the military prisoners, many tens of thousands were shipped out to different parts of the expanding Empire of Japan to work as forced labour.

      After an initial blood-fest by the incoming enemy troops, and some fairly brutal demonstrations aimed at establishing the new order of superiority of victor over vanquished, for a great many of the prisoners life on the island settled back briefly into a relatively relaxed period. There were a number of different prison camps on the island where the military prisoners were kept. The civilian prisoners were rounded up and initially kept in Changi Gaol. Also in the vicinity of the gaol was a tented area for military prisoners called Changi Camp. Here it seems, the prisoners were in effect able to run things themselves, within certain restrictions. Until early March 1942, prisoners had been at liberty to wander seemingly at will, even to go into Singapore town, but these excursions stopped when three young soldiers, unable to get back from town, were caught, court martialed and executed.

7

CHANGI GAOL 1942-1943

It would be easy, at this distance from events, to become caught up in the details, negative and positive, that the unique situation of being a prisoner of war in Changi and the Singapore camps presents. Myriad official and personal accounts exist: some horrific, descriptive of cruelties and degradation, illness and malnutrition; many inspiring, of self-sacrifice and heroism. The details surrounding Tommie Ryan's experience are slim, though those few that do exist, coupled with an observation of the path his life followed after liberation, allow us to view his life from a wider perspective, perhaps allowing us to view a more universal picture, of the common human potential.

Changi camp was a pressure cooker. Whatever was going on in the outside world at the time, was certainly happening on this isolated island in a more intense, concentrated way. The cooking of the human potential, from raw possibility to whatever its designated completion, was happening here at a faster pace. A war was raging in the outside world, a war that was changing and reshaping, not just a geo-political topography, but cultural, social, domestic and individual lives were being turned around within this violent chrysalis of apparent destruction. A world discovering itself anew in the imaginal metamorphosis that marks the evolution of human spirit. Were we to remain with the suffering of the caterpillar, would we ever be able to appreciate the beauty of the butterfly? Yet, all gratitude is due to the one who, in spite of the pain, or perhaps because of it, spurns the ghosts of history and moves on, shedding skins to arrive naked, reborn at the gate of a new world.

Good things, bad things, the whole gamut of human behaviour played itself out during those three and a half long years of captivity. Changi became a micro-climate which allowed some a special kind of transformation where, as if in compensation for the outward hardship, a certain yeast had entered the mix, which would give those whose natures were susceptible the chance to rise and expand beyond the apparent confines of their situation. When body is denied, spirit may come to the fore.

So, paradoxically, for Tommie Ryan, becoming a prisoner of war opened possibilities of which he must hardly have dared to dream. He had been sunk twice. Now once again he found himself castaway. Adrift in this sea of unknown, where was the raft of salvation which would bring him to what as yet undiscovered shore?

Within a few days of the island's surrender, the Japanese soldiers, with their long rifles, invariably with bayonets fixed, had rounded up the remaining European civilians. The men were separated from the women and children, lists were made, and they were marched the fourteen miles from Singapore town to the main prison on the island.

In 1969 Changi Gaol was a forbidding old building, painted grim with inherited memories, glimpsed in dark shadows and dappled with tropical sunlight through the trees as I passed through Singapore as an eighteen-year-old backpacker. I slept the night on the nearby beach, and was woken on Christmas morning - Tommie Ryan's birthday - by Chinese students celebrating with fireworks. They shared their breakfast with me under a gloomy monsoon sky, there by the sea where Singapore airport now stands. The prison itself was demolished in 2000, and a new correction facility has been erected. Incarceration, canings ('judicial corporal punishment') and executions continue to take place.

But in 1942, Changi Gaol had only been open for six years, the pride of the Straits Settlements prison service. It had been built by American engineers and modeled on the infamous US prison, Sing Sing. Now, with the arrival of the Imperial Japanese Army, the Royal Coat of Arms above the entrance gates was boarded over. Designed to accomodate six hundred civilian prisoners, Changi now had to fit three thousand men and around four hundred women and children. The military prisoners were accomodated in camps in the surrounding area and the nearby Selarang Barracks. The cells in Changi Gaol were approximately 6 feet by 8 feet. Each cell had a concrete plinth in the centre for a single bed. Other prisoners had to sleep in the narrow space either side. Eventually wire netting was strung across the well between the floors to add more space for sleeping. In practice many prisoners took whatever bedding they possessed and slept outside. There was a small window to the outside, a foot square, and a hole in the floor for a toilet. A photo on Wikipedia clearly shows high level toilet cisterns in the outside passageway feeding into each cell, with three inmates poking heads out of each cell doorway. The cell doors were not locked and many more prisoners were accomodated in the passageways outside. (http://en.wikipedia.org/wiki/File:Allied_prisoners_of_war_after_the_liberation_of_Changi_Prison,_Singapore_-_c._1945.jpg)

The organisation of the prison, the cooking, looking after supplies, internal discipline etc. was left to the prisoners themselves. Committiees were set up in each block and people were elected to head up the various areas of responsibility. The following list of 'rules' issued in October 1942 to prisoners by the camp leader on behalf of the Japanese captors gives some idea of the nature of the way the camp was organised, at least during the first year:

Orders Issued by Camp Supervisor

1) All enemy civil subjects will be interned in Changi Prison Camp;
2) They will do all the necessary work inside Changi Prison camp for their own welfare;
3) The behavior and attitude of the internees toward the Nipponese authorities must be obedient and respectful;
4) The camp will be divided into two camps: the men's camp and the women's camp. Each camp shall have its own hospital.

Its divisions will be settled by the Camp Supervisor on the recommendation of the Camp Executive Committees.

5) All orders of the Camp Supervisor and the Camp Executive Committees shall be obeyed; the daily life of the camp be properly organized;

6) Each Camp, i.e. Men's and Women's, shall elect a representative who will be appointed by the Nipponese authorities. The Men's Representative and the Women's Representative shall be assisted by an Executive Committee elected within their respective camps;

7) In the Women's Camp no lights are to be switched on until 7:30. Roll Call is to be completed by 8:45. Absentees are to be reported to the Nipponese Command Officer immediately. Breakfast 8:50; lunch 12:45; supper 5.45 pm. Lights out 10 pm. By order of the Nipponese high Command) Silence hours is 2:30 to 3:30.

8) Communication between Men's and Women's Camps is strictly prohibited except that approved ministers of religion accompanied by interpreters may visit the Women's Camp for prayers on Sundays and on such other occasions as may be permitted by the Camp Supervisor;

9) No internee shall approach the Nipponese authorities direct, but shall do so through the Men's and Women's Representative respectively.

10) When any Nipponese Officers come into the Camp or into the rooms, internees much bow and stand to attention in their presence. Only those who are sick or aged may remain seated or in bed. Care must be taken to ensure that there is strict

compliance with these orders.

11) Discipline and fire precautions are to be the responsibility of the Camp Committee.

12) No internees are allowed of out of the camp except

a) for the purpose of carrying out such work as may be ordered by the Camp Supervisor

b) for transfer to Miyako Hospital when sick

c) for sea bathing once a month

d) by special permission of the Camp Supervisor. Sentries will accompany all parties proceeding outside the Camp.

13) Cooking for the women's camp will be carried out in the Main Kitchen; Particular care must be taken that infants and children are fed well.

14) Fatigue parties will be provided as necessary both for internal duties and as may be required by the Nipponese authorities except that Internees shall not be called upon to undertake work that may aid the Nipponese war effort.

15) A report of admissions and discharges to and from the Camp Hospital and the Miyako Hospital is to be submitted daily to the Camp Supervisor.

16) Facilities and granted for dental treatment for female patients and other consultants are allowed to visit the Camp at the request of a Lady Medical Officer.

Changi 21st of September. Received from W. Asahi on 31.10.42

(http://www.tighsolas.ca/page477.html)

It has not been possible to verify exactly when the Empress of Asia's catering crew began to do hospital work. In fact, it is likely that most of the able-bodied men were forced to do 'fatigues' outside the prison, such as collecting wood for the cooking. Tommie Ryan seems to have remained working, if not entirely, then certainly for much of his three and a half years in Changi, within the prison hospital system. It is most likely that he would have been working in the British Hospital within the Roberts Barracks where all the barracks had been converted into one big sick bay with operating theatre and isolation wards.

Many of the great and the good of pre-war colonial Singapore and Malaya had been interned along with Tommie and his shipmates from the Empress of Asia. Among the foremost was the renowned educationalist Harold R Cheeseman, who before his retirement had been a teacher at the elite Penang Free School - where the first president of Malaya, Tunku Abdul Rahman was educated – and later he was Inspector of Schools Penang, and then Deputy Director for Education in the Straits Settlements and Examinations Secretary. Another ex-headmaster from Penang Free School interned in Changi was D R Swaine.

According to Cheeseman's own report made after the war, he was summoned by the Japanese shortly after arrival in Changi Prison, and put in charge of education for boys under the age of 16 years. He became the Camp Education Officer for the duration of their internment. It would seem that some guardian angel was keeping an eye on Tommie. Perhaps due to his small size, and young age - he was barely sixteen when taken prisoner - he was included in whatever educational programmes developed. Although he did spend his allotted work periods helping in the hospital, he was admitted among a small group of mostly slightly younger lads, and able to restart his schooling which had been interrupted a couple of years earlier.

The schooling was wide and varied. The camp contained experts in many fields, and up until 10 October 1943, the labour duties were light for civilians, which meant that there was plenty of free time. The choice, it seems, was either to be bored or to learn something, and at one point there were as many as 2,000 prisoners attending classes in all sorts of subjects. The classes were taught by fellow inmates who either had been teachers prior to their incarceration, or were simply experts in a particular field of interest and eager to pass on their knowledge. Most of the classes took place in the open air, often sitting on the ground. Classes also took place in the women's section of the prison during this period.

Another student at this time was young Eric de Broise Dietz, a couple of years younger than Tommie, whose family were second generation Europeans in the Far East. In time Tommie and Eric were to become fast friends and met on occasion back in the UK after the war ended. Eric wrote later that the only snag about school in a prison camp was that it made truancy impossible!

One of the few personal documents which exist relating to this period in Tommie's life is the following school report, signed by the above mentioned D R Swaine as Changi School's headmaster:

CHANGI SCHOOL

REPORT FOR THE FIRST TERM OF 1943 OF THOMAS RYAN
UPPER FORM
MARKS: 487   PLACE FOR FORM: 3/3

SUBJECTS	MARKS%	REMARKS
ENGLISH	56	GOOD AVERAGE WORK. GRAMMAR WEAK. SHOWS PROMISE
Arithmetic	49	WEAK. IRREGULAR HOMEWORK. LACKS CONCENTRATION.
ALGEBRA	41	
GEOMETRY	46	QUITE CAPABLE. MUST DO BETTER.
FRENCH	59	GOOD WORK DONE. KEEN BUT LACKS STEADINESS
GEOGRAPY	46	FAIR KNOWLEDGE OF FACTS. COULD DO BETTER.
HYGEINE	63	GOOD
HISTORY	65	PROMISING. SHOULD CONCENTRATE ON TIDY ARRANGEMENT
RELIGIOUS KNOWLEDGE	62	KEEN BUT NOT MAKING THE NECESSARY EFFORTS TO LEARN

A good term's work though there is room for improvement in Algebra and Geography.

Tommy's progress has been steady and with a little more application there will be far more improvement. He is ambitious and his return to school after an absence of some time is praiseworthy. He has a good future before him if he keeps on plodding and maintains his interest in his studies. Has powers of leadership.

D R Swaine

Headmaster.

30-4-43

* * *

It is not difficult to read between the lines of this interesting document to get a sense of the state of young Tommie at this time. There is evidently a degree of struggle going on, caused by any number of factors, including, no doubt, that of puberty. 'Quite capable. Must do better' - remarks so familiar in teenage boys school reports since time immemorial. The poor diet too, would not help concentration. But the psychological boost he would have received due to the encouragement from his new role models must have been tremendous. What better compensation for the situation he found himself in than the chance to learn. And what a positive picture it presents of the attitude of his teacher and mentor, Mr Swaine, who, in spite of the circumstances, is able to tell him he has a good future before him. One imagines the good Mr Swaine as a kind of Mr Chips, able to keep his head, both literally and in the Kipling sense, while maintaining a positive morale among his charges.

8

SELARANG INCIDENT AND THE DOUBLE TENTH

In this large, enclosed community - a prison rightly termed a 'concentration camp' such as Singapore had now become, cut off from outside sources of news - boredom was one of the more obvious results. This lead in turn to a whole universe of misinformation and rumours which circulated the camps in lieu of fact-based news. From time to time, however, events occurred which, while not directly involving Tommie Ryan, had serious consequences for all prisoners.

The first of these was the Selarang Barracks incident. The Selarang Barracks was nearby Changi Prison. It had been a British Army barracks and now was the main accomodation for the British and Australian military prisoners of war. In August 1942 Selarang held around 17,000 men. Following a failed escape attempt by four soldiers from the camp, on 30 August the POWs were requested to sign a pledge not to escape. They refused *en masse*, as this was a contravention of the Geneva Convention (to which Japan was not a signatory). The Japanese commander then had the whole camp corralled in the barracks square, an area about 400 ft by 650 ft, with no sanitation and only one tap. After three days the POWs had not given in so the Commandant had the four escapees executed by firing squad. Still the prisoners maintained their stance, in spite of growing deaths through dysentry, until the prisoners' commander, Lt-Gen Holmes, ordered them to sign 'under duress'. Then they signed, but many gave false names. A *nom de plume* favoured by the Australian soldiers was 'Ned Kelly'. After signing, the prisoners were allowed back into their usual quarters.

The other incident was the infamous 'Double Tenth' which had a much more direct and lasting effect on the life of Tommie and the civilian prisoners. I remember when I was a child, each year on 10th October were we warned by our mother to steer clear of our father. We were not really sure why – something to do with his being a POW in Changi. Gradually some small, confused details came out, about his being forced to stand at attention with all the other prisoners, in the hot sun, all day from morning to night. Prisoners who collapsed were beaten and made to get back on their feet.

If on that day he had to write the date, on cheques etc. he would write it with two X's, like two crosses, the Roman numeral for ten. I guess it was a kind of morbid ritual, sad and self-pitying perhaps, but for him a necessary reminder of the suffering of that time, the strange cross he was determined to bear in grim silence. Remembering these small things now makes me wish he had been able to tell his own story. But as he wasn't able to then, it seems right nonetheless that some attempt to uncover it now may, with love and compassionate understanding, throw some light on that sadness, and perhaps loosen the knots tied deep in his soul so long ago.

In fact the 'Double Tenth' incident is very well, if harrowingly, documented, as it figured prominently in the Japanese War Crimes Trials held immediately after the war.

It is a curious thing how so many events, appearing initially separately and seemingly completely unconnected, in time link up to build a single, multifaceted picture. I remember a TV movie in the 1980s, 'The Heroes', telling of a real life raid by Australian and British commandos, launching their little kayaks from an old fishing boat and paddling inshore to lay limpet mines on Japanese ships in a harbour somewhere in the East Indies. And I remember that I thrilled as the heroes made their escape to the sound of explosions and sinking ships. Little did I know then what terrible train of events had followed this seeming victory.

The explosions in the nearby naval dockyard would have been heard clearly by the many thousands of prisoners lying that night behind the miles of barbed wire surrounding their camp. As they lay there in the tropical heat, perhaps unable to sleep from the interminable buzzing of mosquitoes, did they let out a quiet cheer themselves as they let their imaginations run to what might have taken place?

This was in fact the famous 'Operation Jaywick', named for a brand of toilet cleaner, a covert sabotage action carried out by Allied commandos in a captured Japanese fishing boat, renamed 'Krait' (after the small but deadly snake found in the East

Indies, and also popular in literature, appearing in the writings of Conan Doyle, Rudyard Kipling and Roald Dahl). Led by the larger than life Captain Ivan Lyon, a British SOE officer who reputedly had a tiger tattoed on his chest, they set off from Exmouth in West Australia. Twenty-four days later the team reached the environs of Singapore. From a forward base about thirty miles short of their target, six men set off in folding canoes and on the night of 26th September 1943 they laid limpet mines on Japanese oil tankers in Keppel Harbour. Seven ships, totalling 39,000 tons, were destroyed. The commandoes were undetected and returned safely to Exmouth Gulf.

The Japanese in Singapore, never imagining that the attack could have been anything other than an act of internal sabotage, exacted a severe revenge upon the civilian and POW population of the island. On the morning of 9 October, the inmates of Changi Prison were all ordered outside into the courtyard at 9 a.m. Not having eaten since 6 pm on the previous evening, the prisoners were forced to stand at attention all day in the sun without food or drink. The Japanese soldiers carried out a meticulous search of the prison, ransacking the place from top to bottom in their efforts to find evidence linking prisoners to the attack in the harbour.

Some radios were discovered, as well as diaries and notes of broadcasts. A number of people were removed for questioning. In all a total of fifty-seven prisoners were taken away in the following six months and questioned by the 'Kempetai', the Japanese military police. The prisoners were brutally and continually tortured over many months. In at least fifteen cases the torture lead to the prisoners' deaths. There had, in fact, been no collaboration between any of the internees and the outside saboteurs. The radios which had been discovered had been used solely to listen to the BBC and provide a secret news service within the prison.

The 'Double Tenth' incident resulted in the closing down of the school in the camp, and increased labour duties for the prisoners.

The accumulation of actions, and the experiences undergone by a human being in his or her life does not have its results, its rewards or punishments, only for that particular person. We are of a single origin and although we may delude ourselves that we can act out our lives independently of each other, the pretense of autonomy collapses at moments of great tragedy or great celebration. What the efforts of our forefathers and mothers bequeath us are but steps in the continuous journey of the evolution of the human spirit. Sometimes it seems that little if any progress takes place over countless generations, at other times great leaps are taken, at great expense to those involved in the moment - leaps fully into the unknown taken perhaps as desperate measures when it might seem as if the whole future of humanity may be at stake.

World War One, while it did break down the old imperiao orders of Europe and the Middle East, can perhaps be considered as only a preparation, a ploughing of the earth for seeding, to loosen a little the joints of the body while actually being only make-over, an adjustment of the maquillage of moribund governments and social attitudes. The World War of 1939-1945 was the first struggle to take place on a truly global scale, a war which changed irreversably the groundplan for the future. So it would be shortsighted to view the effects of this conflict and make judgements simply in terms of the suffering and destruction that was visited upon all parties in this conflict, whether their participation was active or passive, right or wrong.

That the generations that have followed, the children, the grandchildren and the future generations unborn, owe an immeasurable debt to the past is something we perhaps take for granted in this age of so obvious materialism. Such sentiments have been reduced to platitudes as time turns to distant history these events which produced real and permanent change in the psyche of the planet. In view of the impending world crises - the inescapable facts of climate change; population growth; increased longevity in developed nations; reduced life-expectancy in failing states; global arms proliferation; and the current global pandemic, to mention the most obvious signs of change - there is much to be learnt from the way our parents behaved, their pain, their struggle and their certainty, in their own era of emergency.

The exigencies of wartime encouraged an atmosphere of selflessness in the face of the immediate and present danger; and that selflessness, the collapse of imagined autonomies, produced the materia for actions so much bigger than the individual person, actions aided by a uniting of spirit - or even, the action of a single spirit - to overcome the 'evils' which had arisen like so many hydra-heads claiming their autonomies like cancers in various parts of the body of this earth.

    Within the climate of such a struggle Tommie Ryan too underwent his own personal metamorphosis. Working in Roberts Barracks hospital, Tommie would have witnessed all manner of medical treatment. The hospital dealt with all cases, civil and military, and would have brought him in contact with many notable medical people of the time. There were more than two hundred doctors interned in Singapore, with specialists in many fields. One in particular was the biochemist Dr John W Field CMG, MD. John Field was already a world authority on malaria when he became a civilian prisoner of war in Singapore. He had been Malaria Research Officer at the Institute for Medical Research in Kuala Lumpur since 1931, and in post-war years became the Director of the Institute. Tommie had worked as an assistant under him for a month sometime in 1944/45, where he had intimated to his superior that he intended to study for a medical career. In a reference letter given to Tommie shortly after the liberation of Singapore, John Field had written:

'This is to state that Mr Thomas Ryan has assisted in the Pathological Laboratory of this Camp for a month during a vacation from his matriculation classes. He showed an enthusiastic interest in the Laboratory routine and a ready willingness to make himself useful. He intends, I understand, to study for a medical career. I believe from what I have seen of him that he would make a keen and successful student.'

But hospital work wasn't all messing round with test-tubes and bunsen burners. The hospital survived the internment with the equipment which had been brought in at the time of the island's surrender. The few surgical instruments were supplemented by improvised tools made from kitchen cutlery; there was little if anything in the way of medical supplies such as morphine, bandages etc. Any available rags of material were used to make bandages, which were boiled after use and re-used again and again. Botanists were able to extract some medicines from local herbs, and home-made splints and crutches were fashioned by prisoners in-house. The floors of the barrack-room hospital were covered in sand, like sawdust in a north of England pub, but rarely was it refreshed. Hospital beds were simply boards, and there were no mosquito nets. In the wet heat of the tropics, organic growth was swift, and always there was the disgusting reek of the effects of human illness to contend with. Dysentery was endemic and often a killer. Malnutrition was the most common ailment, from which no one was immune. The civilian prisoners had begun internment on the same rations as were provided for the Japanese soldiers. However, as the war progressed, and supplies diminished, these were reduced. Rations were only provided to those who worked, and although those who had food shared it with the weak and the ill, it meant less all round.

In 1971, I visited my father at his request in Pretoria, South Africa. In a rare moment of paternal candour, he opened up to me, briefly, on a personal matter relating to his time in Changi.

'It was Sunday,' he said, 'and I was attending Mass in the little chapel in the prison camp. I went up to the altar to receive Holy Communion. At the moment the priest placed the host on my tongue, an extraordinary thing happened. I found myself looking down from the roof of the chapel, seeing myself below. I watched myself get up from the altar rail and walk back and kneel down at my seat. In that instant I knew with certainty that I was going to become a doctor. Then I found myself back in my body again.' However we may wish to explain, interpret or question this curious incident, the proof, as they say, is in the pudding, as future events were to show.

Following the events which culminated in the 'Double Tenth' incident, the Japanese authorities put an end to the whole prison educational programme which Harold Cheeseman had set up. Nevertheless, teaching for the boys, and in the women's camp for the girls, continued in a clandestine fashion. It had been the aim of Cheeseman and his colleagues to continue to prepare some young students to take the Cambridge School Certificate while in the camp. Cheeseman wrote later that 'as much as possible was done surreptitiously for the boys, who were taken individually in sequestered corners of the Prison'. (H.R.Cheeseman, A Brief Review of the Educational Programme in the Singapore Internment Camp. University of Cambridge)

On 1 May 1944 the civilian internees were moved out of Changi Gaol in order to make room for an influx of military prisoners of war returning to Singapore after working as slave labour on the notorious Burma/Thailand railway. Around 3,000 civilians, Tommie among them, were transferred to a site at Sime Road, a former British air force camp just a few miles north-west of Singapore Town. By the war's end the camp held just over 4,500 prisoners, including 1,023 women and 328 children. While most of those held there were British, the Sime Road camp also became home to members of twenty-six other nationalities including many Eurasians, as well as Australians, Jews, Chinese and Polish detainees.

In Sime Road Camp the school continued to provide teaching to a small group of children, including Tommie Ryan. In July 1944 permission was granted to 're-open' the school - notwithstanding that it had been teaching in secret since the Double Tenth, in the manner of the Catholic 'hedge schools' in 18th century Ireland. The school was divided into 'Upper' and 'Lower' schools. Tommie was among only eleven pupils in the Upper School, as the older boys were required by the Japanese to do day labour, as much as six hours a day. Already suffering from malnutrition due to the meagre rations, many of those eligible for schooling must have been just too tired to concentrate on studying.

Harold Cheeseman continued preparing the small group for the School Certificate Examination, with the aim of holding exams in December 1944 for those who were ready. In the event, the exams were held in January 1945 for seven candidates, and in August 1945 for three candidates, just one day before news came of the Japanese surrender. Two of the candidates were girls from the adjoining women's camp.

The results of the first exam were given out to the students in February 1945, and a short article in The Straits Times after the war (18th December 1945) confirmed that the exam results had been ratified by the University of Cambridge Local Examination Syndicate. The article said that the newspaper had *'received a notice from Major D. Roper Education Officer, BMA (Singapore) stating that certificates for the Cambridge School Certificate Examination are awaiting Clifford H. Bolton, Max Brisk, Eric Albert de Broise Dietz, <u>Thomas C. Ryan</u>, Charles B. N. Symons and Mary Winters, in his office.'* It was after discovering this article on a website for digitalised newspapers which enabled me to make contact and eventually meet up with Eric de Broise's widow, Ivy, and one of his daughters, Anne, in 2012, seventy years after Tommie and Eric had first met.

Tommie seems to have had an insatiable appetite for knowledge of all kinds. In later adulthood he was quite capable of reading a book a day, and often did, mostly thrillers, modern history and politics, and medicine of course, but he went through periods of interest in art and to some extent religion. One room in our house in Perth was given over entirely to books. He was also an avid listener to classical music and light opera, and he built up a large collection of box sets of long playing records. He was particularly fond of Bach and Mahler, as well as Mozart, Beethoven, Brahms - all the greats in fact. He also was also able to play the piano, by ear.

In the early 1960s he purchased a piano, a baby-grand, where in the evening when he came in from the surgery he would unwind, playing away for twenty or thirty minutes, tunes from the latest musicals, tunes he remembered from the past. He just played away, usually with a degree of gusto, rolling chords up and down the octaves, until our mother brought in his supper on a tray, which he would eat, sitting in his armchair while at the same time consuming a fat paperback thriller.

Where his interest in music began is anyone's guess, but where had he learnt to play?

'In the prison camp,' he told us children, 'there was a dummy piano, just the keys, no strings. So I had to imagine the tunes in my head and I learn to play the notes without sound on the keyboard.' I always thought it something of a minor miracle that he could just play away on the piano without any apparent musical education. But he was like that. If something interested him, it seemed he could absorb the essentials like blotting paper. Something of this natural ability must have propelled him through the learning process in the prison camp, particularly in the practical aspects of the work in the hospital. He was always a hands-on doctor, loved surgery, midwifery, talking to the patient; the details of medicine facinated him and he tried to pass on his enthusiasm to me, but without success. He would demonstrate anatomy to me with a human skull in hand, pointing out the various grooves and indents and explaining the names according to their Latin meanings. I enjoyed the Latin, but had little interest in the skull. Intellectually he was certainly bright, but not what is termed a high-flyer in the academic sense, and had trouble with exams in later years.

It cannot have been easy for Tommie's mother during his long period of incarceration, as news of Tommie's situation only filtered out to her bit by bit. The first official notification she received from Canadian Pacific Steamships regarding her son was a bland piece of printed bureaucracy stating *'with regret'* that *'the ship on which your (*and here a gap into which the word *son* has been typed*) was serving has been lost. We do, however, have information that all the crew were safely landed at Singapore, but no advice has been received regarding your (son) since the 5th February.'* There then follows a couple of paragraphs about payment of Dependents Allowances. Nowhere does it mention Tommie's name, nor, strangely, the name of his ship. We imagine that news of such a big loss as that of the Empress of Asia was public knowledge by then, and Sarah would have been worrying about her Tommie for some time. It was not until more than a year later, in a further letter, dated 1st June 1943, from the Canadian Pacific Catering Department, at 1 Gladstone Dock, just down the road from her rented accommodation in Liverpool 8, that the following cryptic piece of information was revealed to her:

'*Dear Mrs Ryan,*

this is to inform you that advice has been received that THOMAS RYAN, Engineers' Boy, "Empress of Asia", has been reported by the International Red Cross Society as being a Prisoner of War at Changi Camp, Singapore.'

As early as July 1942, prisoners in Changi had been issued with postcards by the Japanese with strict instructions on how they were to be filled in: typed, with no complaints, no hidden messages etc. One postcard to his mother, one of only two that Tommie wrote, or at least the only two that reached its destination, was sent with the date 1st November 1942. The postcard is typed and signed in pencil 'Tommie'. In it he says that she is now allowed to write to him, care of The Red Cross. It is unlikely that it reached its destination before the above letter from the CP Catering Department. A document in the archives of the International Red Cross in Geneva refers to a telegram sent by Japanese authorities on 11th May 1943 confirming that 'Mr Thomas Ryan, Merchant Seaman, Age 16,' was a British civilian interned in Changi Camp. The Japanese were not signatories to the Geneva Convention with regard to Prisoners of War.

Throughout all this time little hard news found its way in or out of the prison island of Singapore. Rumours of victories and defeats in the wider theatre of the war circulated wildly. These were rarely accurate, though they might contain a thread of truth wrapped in much fearful conjecture or wishful thinking. The impulse of Japanese expansion had been blunted relatively early, in May and June 1942 following the sea battles of the Coral Sea, just north of Australia, and Midway in mid-Pacific Ocean. From then on a long war of attrition on both sides was fought year after years as American and ANZAC forces whittled away at the enemy on many fronts in the Pacific and Indian Ocean regions, gradually closing the net on Japan itself.

In June 1944, American forces captured the Mariana Islands, on the eastern corner of the triangle that is the Phillipine Sea, with Tokyo in the north, New Guinea in the south, and Manila in the west. This gave the USAAF the necessary forward base to launch long-range bombing attacks into Japan itself. It was from an airfield on the island of Tinian in the Marianas that the two B-29s took off in August 1945 to drop atom bombs on Hiroshima and Nagasaki.

By October 1944, the effective Japanese fleet had been much reduced, while the US Navy had increased its air arm considerably since Pearl Harbour. Since the sinking of the HMS Hood and KMS Bismarck early in the Atlantic war, aircraft carriers had replaced battleships to become the weapon of choice for sea combat. Sea battles now took place in which the shipboard combatants might never come into visual contact.

Things came to a head with the US invasion of the Philippines on 20th October 1944, led by General Douglas MacArthur. This precipitated the largest naval battle in history, the Battle of Leyte Gulf, during the following week. The combined US and Australian fleet numbered over 300 vessels (including 34 aircraft carriers with 1,500 planes, 12 battleships, 24 cruisers, 141 destroyers and frigates, plus submarines and torpedo boats). At this stage in the war, the Imperial Japanese Navy could only summon up a much smaller force, which included 33 capital ships and in excess of 300 planes. It is notable that here for the first time 'kamikaze' suicide attacks were made by planes. In the ensuing battle, Allied forces lost 3 aircraft carriers and 3 destroyers. More than 200 planes were shot down and around 3,000 sailors, airmen and marines were killed. The Japanese lost half their capital ships, including three huge battleships, ten cruisers and at least nine destroyers, with losses of around 10,500 men. It was a disaster for the Japanese. The remnants of their great battle fleet limped off in two directions, some ships returning to naval bases in the Inland Sea in Japan, while the rest sailed for Lingga Island, just a few miles south of Singapore. From the roof of Changi Gaol, allied PoWs could see the naval dockyards in the Johore Strait to the north of the island. They witnessed the battered IJN fleet entering harbour and the news of a Japanese defeat spread in the camp.

In a reprise to the commando raid in 1943 that precipitated the events of the 'Double Tenth', on 10th October 1944, the Allies undertook 'Operation Rimau', to sink Japanese shipping at Singapore. Again led by Lt. Col. 'Tiger' Lyon, this time things went badly wrong. Although some vessels were sabotaged, four members of the team were killed in or as a result of action, and ten members, including Lyon, were captured, put on trial for espionage and subsequently beheaded.

9

FREED FROM THE NOOSE

'They were drunken, freed from the noose' – Rumi

Singapore, 6:44 am, 5th November 1944.

In the misty freshness of a November morning in the tropics, the residents of Sime Road Camp, were in the process of arising and preparing a breakfast from what little rations were available. The prisoners in Changi Gaol, similarly responding to their various muted reveilles and calls of nature, were making their way to their alotted work details, or simply lying abed, ill and listless from the effects of malnutrition. The Chinese civilians of the island, those that had survived the massacres and imprisonments, after lifting the shutters of their shops, were sprinkling water to lay the dust while sweeping the pavement in front. The Malays in their kampongs, were up and about, preparing what meagre rice or tapioca they could find for breakfast. Even the garrison and commanders of the occupying forces were awake and at their posts. All now heard the thunder sounds high in the sky, welcome for some, doomladen for others, which clarified into the dull throb of aeroplane engines followed by the hollow, echoing crump of distant bombs.

The date chosen for the first Allied bombing raid on Singapore was, somewhat ironically, Guy Fawkes Day. Seventy-six

B-29 'Superfortress' bombers of XX Bomber Command of the United States Army Air Forces took off from Kharagpur Airfield in West Bengal, India, and flew the nearly-2,000 miles down the Bay of Bengal, each carrying two 1,000 bombs. The target was the Singapore Naval Base – specifically, the King George Graving Dock - where damaged ships from the Battle of Leyte Gulf were being repaired. A number of direct hits put the dockyard out of action for three months.

After nearly three years of waiting, the news that they were not forgotten and that help was finally at hand must have been a tremendous boost to the prisoners' morale. Further massive bombing raids, of shipping in Singapore docks, as well as the repair yards, and oil supply depots on surrounding islands took place from January 1945, through February up to the end of March. In addition, on every full moon until the end of May, B-29s and R.A.F. B-24 'Liberator' bombers were used to lay mines in the sea lanes surrounding Singapore. Significant damage to the Japanese military supply chain through the Malay Peninsula was effected both on land and at sea. The Japanese anti-aircraft defenses were poor and only nine American planes were lost during this bombing campaign.

Then in early August, a Royal Navy midget submarine operation penetrated Singapore Harbour and laid limpet mines on Japanese warships, seriously damaging the cruiser Takao.

Following the dropping of the atom bombs on Hiroshima and Nagasaki on 6th and 9th August 1945, the Japanese Emperor

Hirohito, finding the war had 'not gone to our advantage', gave the order to surrender on 15th August.

This order was not immediately appreciated in Singapore by its commander, General Itagaki Seishiro, who with many of his officers and men had vowed to fight to the death, and he only ordered his men to surrender on 20th August after conferring with his overall commander in Saigon, thus averting the feared massacre of the Allied PoWs.

Still, it was a tense time as everybody waited for an official statement. For Tommie and the residents of Sime Road Camp it came on 24th August in a 'Special Announcement' by camp representatives who after a meeting with the Japanese informed the prisoners that the war was over but negotiations for the handover of Singapore were in progress, with British troops expected to arrive at the beginning of September. This announcement included a long list of welcome changes in the order of things, in marked contrast to the draconian regulations then in force, and those earlier Camp Orders issued in October 1942. The first measure, giving an indication of the priorities of the time, was the abolition of all smoking and lighting restrictions. Throughout the announcement the Japanese are openly referred to as 'The Nips', as in *'The Nips will endeavour to send in supplies of eggs and fish...The Nips will endeavour to send us supplies of boots and shoes for both camps.'* Planes would be flying over the following day dropping food and supplies which were to be collected, checked and made available. Restraint was called for from the internees, and *'in the interest of safety of all of us, no internee should give the slightest provocation that might cause an incident between the Camp and the Nips.'*

    Then, almost without noticing, it was all over. The Japanese soldiers vanished from the camp. One day planes appeared in the sky, and British soldiers in parachutes began to float down. Then, on 28th August, airdrops of food and medicines began. The internees were still kept in the camp for a while, but gradually a different order, or perhaps disorder, began to unfold, and trips out to town were made.

    On 5th September the Royal Navy arrived, the cruiser HMS Sussex leading a huge flotilla of troop ships, hospital ships, aircraft carriers, landing craft and all manner of cargo ships. Thousands of Allied troops flooded the island, dispensing the longed-for largesse of cigarettes, tea and bread, medicines and security, as well as a different kind of law and order than that meted out for the past three and a half years. It was now the turn of the Japanese to be disarmed and interned. While the civilian population and the newly-liberated POWs errupted in joy with the arrival of the liberating fleet, for the Japanese, now being interned and processed prior to trials for war crimes, it was a time of deep shame. For some Japanese officers it was too much to bear, and rather than surrender, three hundred committed suicide by hand-grenade in the Raffles Hotel. Then Lord Louis Mountbatten, who was the Supreme Allied Commander in the South East Asia Command, arrived in Singapore for the formal signing of the surrender document which took place at the Municipal Hall on 12th September.

About a week later, Tommie Ryan, along with 950 military and merchant marine personel was aboard SS Nieuw Holland, one of the first repatriation ships to leave Singapore. On board were the internees from the crew of Empress of Asia, many of them from Liverpool and now collectively known as "the Asia Boys".

10

FORTUNES OF WAR

SS Nieuw Holland was met by cheering crowds in Liverpool docks on 15th October after a voyage of around three and a half weeks, sailing via Colombo and Suez. Back on Merseyside, the ex-PoWs were first given medicals and taken to a transit camp on the Wirral Peninsula from where Tom Ryan was able to send his mother a brief telegram: "ARRIVED SAFELY SEE YOU SOON = TOMMY NO 76 TRANSIT-CAMP EASTHAM WIRRAL". Now the spelling of his name has graduated to 'Tommy', perhaps to save money as telegrams were charged by the letter; or being nineteen years of age, he considered it more manly.

  It was four years less four weeks since he had sailed out of the Mersey aboard Empress of Asia. His hair, then a reddish-brown, now darkened to almost black, and he no longer contained within the 5 foot 2 inches of height as shown in his seaman's Discharge Certificate. In spite of the privations suffered, he now topped out at 5 foot 8 ½ inches. It was four years since he had seen his mother, now remarried to Mr Tone, giving Tommy another sister, Pat, and later a brother William. Would she have recognised her firstborn? He had changed.

  Somewhere in all the excitement of his arrival, he was buttonholed by a reporter from the Liverpool Daily Post. The paper's issue next day contained an item headlined: BOY "DOCTOR" OF SINGAPORE - LIVERPOOL YOUTH'S EXPERIENCE -

PRISON CAMP STUDIES. The article began *'Few medical students have started their training in grimmer circlumstances than nineteen-years-old Thomas Christopher Ryan, of 101 Ponsonby Street, Liverpool, one of the repatriated men who disembarked from the Netherlands liner Nieuw Holland in Liverpool yesterday after being delayed at the Bar by fog for seven and a half hours. His story, given to a Daily Post reporter, tells of long-cherished ambition that by the fortunes of war, now gives promise of fulfillment.'* The article outlined his childhood dreams, his war history and his future aspirations in the field of medicine. Tommy was casting his line out having barely set his feet on home shores. As fortune favours the brave, this article was seen by a wealthy Yorkshire widow who subsequently subsidised Tommy during his first couple of years as a medical student at Liverpool University.

In 2008, long after Tommy had qualified, moved to Australia, and from there to South Africa in 1970, an old university friend of Tommy's, David Alltree, a doctor who also emigrated from Liverpool to Perth, published a book, 'The Leaving of Liverpool - Medical Migration to Western Australia'. Chapter Five is dedicated to Tommy Ryan, in which Alltree reveals some interesting details of their time together at University of Liverpool's Medical School:

'I first met (him) in the dissecting room of the Medical School in 1948... Slightly tubby with dark curly hair he had all the attributes of a congenial Irishman although he was born in Liverpool. He had the ability and charm to talk to anyone and he

asked if he could join our group in the dissection of a cadaver we were about to work on.'

Medical school was no easy ride for Tommy, who up until then had done most of his learning by oral instruction. Alltree writes:

'Much of his medical knowledge was gleaned while sitting under the trees in the camp talking to doctors.'

It was only after a number of failed attempts did Tommy finally graduate by passing the Examination of the Worshipful Society of Apothecaries of London.

'Their Finals in 1953 were in April and Tom dutifully passed his final exams and, despite his initial disadvantage, in fact was registered as a Medical Practitioner some three months ahead of the rest of the year. He always had top ability but not the "know how" of the techniques to pass examinations...His registration was a quite remarkable achievement.'

Tommy set up in medical practice in Birkenhead, where he stayed until 1958 when, having applied for a four year commission in the Royal Australian Navy, he was gazetted as a Surgeon Lieutenant and by now married to Patricia McMahon embarked with their four children on the P&O vessel 'Oronsay' to Sydney.

After outlining the rest of his life until Tom's death in South Africa in 1990 (they remained friends during their years together in Perth, and after his departure in 1970), Alltree sums up with a most generous tribute to their joint alma mater and kind encomium to his friend:

'I regard Tom as one of the greatest achievements of our Medical School. To have a boy with no formal education and to watch him over the years achieve the mantle, good standing and social acceptability of a medical practitioner and a useful member of society verges almost on the miraculous. It was a privilege to have known him.'

AFTERWORD

It is commonly accepted that children are a gift to their parents. But I believe the opposite may also be true, that the parents by their actions, efforts and achievments, may be a gift to those that come after. Whatever may or may not occur in later life, the actions of a person's early years, in coming to whatever maturity of possibility may be their lot, define that person's true character. Tom Ryan underwent a baptism of fire on many occasions in his early life. Born into a poor Liverpool Irish family, removed from school at an early age and then becoming fatherless, in dangerous times of war he followed the band regardless of what the future might bring. And for nearly five years, at the most impressionable time of life, he underwent some of the most intense experiences one would ever wish upon anyone: years of adventure and suffering, fear and loss. Yet also not without help and love, so that in time he was built, not just on the outside, but inside as well. And he survived. Certainly not by his own efforts alone - he received immeasurable help from many quarters - but he followed his path and he did make his dream real. He made it to university, he became a doctor, he married and brought into the world four children.

That this world of his then later disintegrated, with marriage breakdown and divorce, and had to be built again, in another place, with other loves and another family, does not invalidate the previous stages. He passed from this life barely a week before his sixty-fifth birthday. He had been a heavy smoker most of his life, had undergone heart surgery in his forties, and no doubt the rigours of recurrent malaria added to the complications that took their final toll. Certainly none of us are perfect, and none of us appear as saints while clothed in the earthly garb of body and desires. But what may appear in time as mistakes, we hope and pray be covered by forgiveness and understanding in the final analysis. Possibilities for progress always remain open after souls emerge beyond the veils of this life.

The gift that Tom Ryan brought cannot easily be measured or defined. In many ways it is part of the same gift which that whole generation of men and women who suffered through the cataclysms of the first half of the 20th century brought to humanity. We have seen the collapse of old social and religious ways as the world moves in fits and starts, by hook or by crook, from insular and divisive political modes, of tribes and warlords, of kindoms and empires, of the dark orders of fascism, and dictatorial communism, as the world lurches fitfully towards the vision of a singularity of human meaning within this great diversity of human potential. The sacrifice which that generation made in World War Two, willingly and or by force of circumstance, was a huge step forward in the interior evolution of humanity. It is a gift that may still unfold in each of us, should we agree to take accept the mantle of service in the way of love.

Tom Ryan, in those five years of his youth, leapt the high fences of convention and birth to land me and his other descendants, in a place free from so many of the apparent limitations of an earlier, more constricted age. And for that we may be unreservedly grateful. And we hope and pray that our own lives too may be a gift, and not a burden, upon those who descend from us, and that the children may be true inheritors of the parent's secret heart.

RMS Empress of Asia

CANADIAN PACIFIC STEAMSHIPS LIMITED.
PIER HEAD.
LIVERPOOL.

LIVERPOOL.
14th May, 1942.

Ref.C.D.1/2.

Dear Madam,

It is with regret we have to inform you that as a result of enemy action the ship on which your son was serving has been lost. We do, however, have information that all the crew were safely landed at Singapore, but no advice has been received regarding your son since the 5th of February. We are making every endeavour to obtain, through the Colonial Office, all possible information concerning the crew.

We have now received instructions that Dependents Allowances will be paid as from 5th February by the Ministry of Pensions.

For the period from 5th February to 6th May inclusive, your allotment has been paid by us, and as the detention allowance will be back-dated to 5th February, it will be necessary for you to sign attached agreement to refund to us the amount of such allotment from the arrears of detention allowance payable by the Ministry of Pensions.

Yours faithfully,

for CANADIAN PACIFIC STEAMSHIPS LTD.

GENERAL AGENT.

Mrs. Sarah Ryan,
101 Ponsonby St.,
Liverpool, 8.

> Changi Internment Camp, SYONAN (Singapore) Malaya.
> 1/11/42. Dear Mother, I am sending you all my love
> and also to Molly, Leo, Joyce and Billy. Give my
> regards to Harold, please do not worry about me for
> I am in the best of health. You are now allowed to
> write to me to the above address c/o The Red Cross.
> Several people have already received parcels and
> letters. I hope that this will reach you on your's &
> Leo's birthdays, but I doubt it. Lots of love,
> THOMAS RYAN

> Dear Mother,
> I am in the best of health and send all my love to you, Molly, Leo, and Billie. Send my best wishes to Jack, and to Joyce. I am attending school here and I would like you to tell Mr. Andrews & Mr. Morrison Mr. Taylor. I am longing to be home with you all, even with all I have to do, at times it becomes most monotonous. We are getting plenty of healthy exercise through the medium of games. e.g. football, swimming, etc.
> Send regards to the family and other friends of mine. I hope you know that you may write to me through the Red Cross and send parcels. The day I come home will be one I will never forget so once more lots of love,
> Your ever loving son,
> Tommie.

Postcards home from captivity, via the Red Cross

CHANGI SCHOOL

REPORT FOR THE FIRST TERM OF 1945 OF THOMAS RYAN.   UPPER FORM.

MARKS: 467.   PLACE FOR FORM: 3/5.

SUBJECTS	MARKS%	REMARKS.
ENGLISH	56	GOOD AVERAGE WORK. GRAMMAR WEAK. SHOWS PROMISE.
Arithmetic	49	WEAK. IRREGULAR HOMEWORK.
ALGEBRA	41	LACKS CONCENTRATION.
GEOMETRY	16	QUITE CAPABLE. MUST DO BETTER.
FRENCH	59	GOOD WORK DONE. KEEN BUT LACKS STEADINESS.
GEOGRAPHY	16	FAIR KNOWLEDGE OF FACTS. COULD DO BETTER.
HYGIENE	83	GOOD.
HISTORY	85	PROMISING. SHOULD CONCENTRATE ON TIDY ARRANGEMENT.
RELIGIOUS KNOWLEDGE	62	KEEN BUT NOT TAKING THE NECESSARY EFFORTS TO LEARN.

A good term's work though there is room for improvement in Algebra & Geography. Tommy's progress has been steady and with a little more application there will be far more improvement. He is ambitious and his return to school after an absence of some time is praiseworthy. He has a good future before him if he keeps on plodding and maintaining his interest in his studies. Has powers of leadership.

H. R. Swaine
Head Master. 30-4-45

School Report 1945, signed by H.R. Swaine

Exams In Secret

INTERNED BOYS, GIRLS PASS

During the occupation, in the earlier half of 1945, a group of boys and girls surreptitiously sat for the Cambridge School Certificate Examination organized in the Sime Road Internment Camp by the former Deputy Director of Education, Straits Settlements, Mr. H. R. Cheeseman.

Yesterday the Straits Times received a notice from Major D. Roper, Education Officer, B.M.A. (Singapore), stating that certificates for the Cambridge School Certificate Examination are awaiting Clifford H. Bolton, Max Brisk, Eric Albert de Broise Dietz, Thomas C. Ryan, Charles B. N. Symons and Mary Winters, in his office.

The certificates show the standards reached in the separate subjects taken up by the students and include the English language, English literature, religious knowledge, English history, history of the British Empire, elementary mathematics, hygiene and physiology, geography, French and Dutch.

Each certificate bears the following statement: "This was a special examination organized in the Singapore Internment Camp by representatives of the Malayan Education Dept. and later recognised by the University of Cambridge Local Examinations Syndicate." They are all signed by the Vice-Chancellor of the University of Cambridge.

Boris V. Konstantinoff and Nellie Symons should also apply at Major Roper's office in the Municipal Buildings for certificates showing the subjects in which they satisfied the examiners.

From the Straits Times, December 1945

```
                    Sime Road Internment Camp,
                         Singapore,
                              August 26th, 1945.

        THIS is to state that Mr. Thomas Ryan has assisted
    in the Pathological Laboratory of this Camp for a
    month during a vacation from his matriculation classes.
    He showed an enthusiastic interest in the Laboratory
    routine and a ready willingness to make himself useful.
    He intends, I understand, to study for a medical
    career.   I believe from what I have seen of him that
    he would make a keen and successful student.
```

John W Field MD
Institute for
Medical Research
Kuala Lumpur
FMS

Reference for Thomas Ryan signed by Dr John Field CMG

LIVERPOOL DAILY POST. TUESDAY, OCTOBER 16, 1945

BOY "DOCTOR" OF SINGAPORE

LIVERPOOL YOUTH'S EXPERIENCE

PRISON CAMP STUDIES

Few medical students have started their training in grimmer circumstances than nineteen-years-old Thomas Christopher Ryan, of 101 Ponsonby Street, Liverpool, one of the repatriated men who disembarked from the Netherlands liner Nieuw Holland in Liverpool yesterday after being delayed at the Bar by fog for seven and a half hours. His story, given to a *Daily Post* reporter, tells of long-cherished ambition that, by the fortunes of war, now gives promise of fulfilment.

The son of working-class parents, young Ryan lived opposite the Liverpool University, and, watching the familiar sight of white-coated students, was fired with the hope of becoming a doctor.

But, like many of his schoolmates, he drifted into odd jobs and, at fifteen, went to sea as a mess boy in the Canadian Pacific freighter Beaverbrae, which was bombed by a Focker-Wulf and sunk in March, 1941. Picked up by a destroyer he was brought to England and next signed on as a mess boy in the company's Empress of Asia, in which he went trooping to Singapore.

Hospital Volunteer

Again his ship was bombed and sunk, and he was landed in Singapore in time to take part in the battle for that city. Remembering his earlier ambition, Ryan seized his opportunity and volunteered with other shipmates, to work in the general hospital, his first task being the grim business of burying dead. From this he graduated to assisting in rough surgery on the wounded.

Few boys of sixteen have ever been called on to treat the ghastly wounds caused by shell and bomb splinters, but the experience only strengthened Ryan's desire to become a doctor, and when the Japanese finally overran Singapore and he was taken prisoner, he spent every leisure moment in improving his education.

He was so successful in his studies that while still in captivity he succeeded in passing, with honours, for the Cambridge University higher school certificate.

Helped By Doctors

This success prompted him to continue the study of practical medicine. Now home, his earlier enthusiasm burns more brightly than ever, and he is determined to utilise his savings, together with a hoped-for Government grant, in aiming for a future career as a doctor. His studies in the prison camp were aided by many interned chemists and doctors, who fitted up their own pathological laboratory and research rooms.

In all the Nieuw Holland carried 951 Army, Navy, Air Force and Merchant Navy personnel, among the latter being most of the survivors of the Empress of Asia.

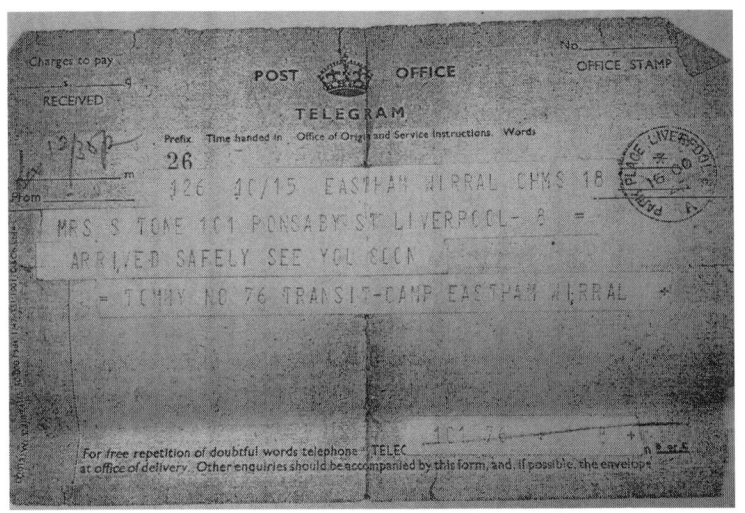

'Arrived Safely' telegram to Tommy's mother

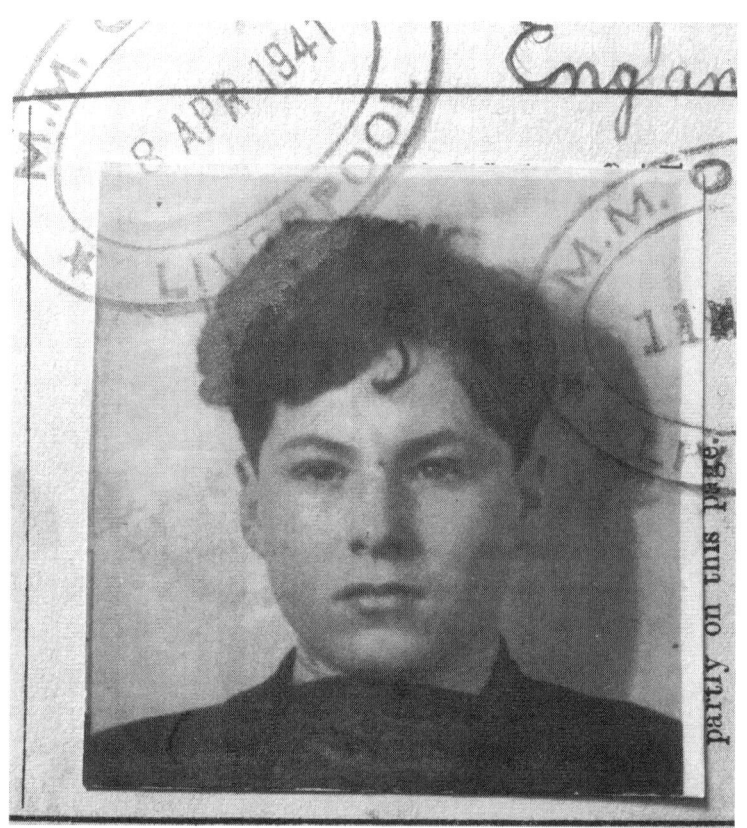

Tommie Ryan aged 15 years

Tommy Ryan, medical student, meeting fellow ex-POW Eric de Broise Dietz and wife Ivy, London c.1952

Surgeon-Lieutenant Thomas Ryan R.A.N., HMAS Creswell, Jervis Bay, ACT, Australia, 1958

Also by Christopher Ryan:

The Story of the Damascus Drum
(248 pp, Hakawati Press,TD9 0AN, Hawick. U.K. - ISBN 978-0-9569552-0-3)

Daud, a successful trader, Takla a young cook, and Shams, an old billy goat from the hills above Damascus take us on a journey of love and self-discovery in time, space, and beyond through the Syrian landscape of the 19th century. An adventure replete with entertaining storytellers recounting tales of mystery and love, villainous villains and hospitable goatherds, clerics both wicked and wise, memorable feasts and a lot of goats....

'A fabulous adventure story, scented with magical realism, resonating with a talking goatskin drum... set among the monuments of Syria, and the old khans and mountainous hinterland of Damascus in a timeless Levant... valued spiritual teachings within a fast-paced plot.'
- Barnaby Rogerson, Eland Books.

'a portrait of the Syria which I recognize as my own country and really miss... takes me to times I have never witnessed, but which my imagination has already visited and lived in."
- Ruba Khadamaljamei - translator at **Syria TV** سوريا تلفزيون

'A journey of self-discovery and rebirth...sympathetic characters who reach out to the living even after their death - a work of Sufi Realism and a beguiling tale...I highly recommend.'
- David Paquiot, SUFI Journal.

'delightful and quirky, it catapults us directly into the old world of Damascus... a magical piece of escapism with a lesson to teach the weary 21st century soul.'
- Marion James, Sunday Zaman, Istanbul.

'profoundly human, funny, wise and it's a good tale.'
- Sebastian Ritscher, Mohrbooks AG, Zürich

(Available in German translation as *'Die Damaszener Trommel'*)

Satanaya and the Houses of Mercy
- The Chronicle of a Circassian Girl
(382 pp, Hakawati Press,TD9 0AN, Hawick. U.K. - ISBN 978-0-9569552-1-0)

Satanaya's adventures as a young girl growing up in *fin-de-siècle* Palestine and Syria, learning her trade as a cook and taking her first steps in the path of love, while discovering an inner world among dervishes on the plains of Anatolia.

" Part travelogue, part romance and part celebration of all things culinary, evoking the ravishing loveliness of the Middle East before the ravages of contemporary conflict -the mood is joyful, playful, sensual, while in the mysterious figure of Captain Mustafa, there are hints of darker shades to come."
- Katherine Tiernan, author of the St Cuthbert trilogy.

" Ryan brilliantly recreates the Middle East in the late 19th and early 20th century... interweaving history, geography, food, and a deep sense of spirituality - contemporary and highly relevant."
 - Martin Gulbis, Steiner Academy

"A book to be savoured, in every sense of the word, for lovers of food and late nineteenth century Middle Eastern history and most importantly the human spirit."
- Norman Latimer, Cornucopia Magazine online

An Ark In The Flood Of Time
- Chronicling the Further Adventures of Satanaya the Circassian
(371 pp, *Hakawati Press,TD9 0AN, Hawick. U.K. - ISBN 978-0-9569552-2-7)*

An Ark in the Flood of Time tells a tale of Satanaya and Mustafa as dark clouds of war descend over Ottoman lands in the early 20th Century. Loves are won and lost, empires dissolve and countries are formed, only to disappear again; identities change as frontiers fall between cities and hearts as fast as fortunes on the roulette wheel. All life is swept up in time's unstoppable current, to be reborn on new and unknown shores...

"There is only one thing to hold onto when all else fails: the being, the existence, the one, God, love, beauty, whatever you call it, however it comes: by taste, intellect, a feeling or a movement of the heart – this is the human reality. You, Satanaya, be certain that it is your boat, your ark, in this flood of time".

'An astonishing achievement by a master wordsmith, a sensuous tale of love,honour and intrigue in the wake of collapsing empires leaving the reader enriched and wiser'
– Richard Gault, Beshara Magazine.

'Beautiful, feisty Satanaya the chef leads us by ancient mystical philosophy through the conflicts of the dying Ottomon Empire. Warmhearted...simmering... humorous... with passages of lyrical beauty in the darkest situations.'
– Elaine Henderson, Potter, B.A.Hons. GSA.

The Author

Christopher Ryan was born in Liverpool, of mostly Irish descent. He was brought up in Australia from the age of seven, returning to Europe overland by way of South East Asia and India. With his wife he set up and ran two restaurants in Cambridge in the 1970s and '80s. Later he spent a year studying Persian and Ottoman Turkish at the University of Oxford before working as a international shipping credit analyst.

In 2000 he helped found Infospectrum Ltd, now, the world's largest independent credit reporting and risk management consultancy in shipping and commodities industries.

His articles on shipping, food, travel and mysticism have been published in Lloyds List, the Financial Times and Cornucopia Magazine, and he has contributed to academic symposia and journals in UK, USA and Turkey.

A perennial student of the Beshara School, he was a director and sometime chairman of the Chisholme Institute, a Scottish educational charity, for 37 years.

Printed in Great Britain
by Amazon